Weekend Fathers

Weekend Fathers

For divorced fathers, second wives
and grandparents—solutions to the
problems of child custody, child support,
alimony and property settlements.

GERALD A. SILVER
and
MYRNA SILVER

Published by
Stratford Press
LOS ANGELES

Distributed by
Harper & Row
NEW YORK

ISBN 0-936906-06-5
Library of Congress Catalog Card 81-51695

MANUFACTURED IN THE UNITED STATES OF AMERICA

To all fathers who are kept from
sharing in the joy and pain
of raising their own children

Contents

viii   Contents

Acknowledgments

The authors wish to acknowledge the untiring efforts of Brad Gilson and Zan Green, who volunteered countless hours of their time in the fight for men's and fathers' rights.

We also would like to thank Carl Bruaw, Mike Stein, Judy and John Mertz, James Cook, Art Raynor, Charles Bishop and Louis Muscate, who put their own personal problems aside to serve on the board of Fathers' Rights of America, Inc. Their dedication has helped many men remain in the lives of their children after divorce.

We also recognize the pioneering work by Vert Vergon of Fathers Demanding Equal Justice and Rod Bivings and Paulis Smith of United Fathers Organization, Inc. Their efforts are bringing hope to many men seeking joint custody of their children.

Finally, we want to thank all those in men's-rights organizations across the nation who are working to change a brutal adversary family-law system into a more humane method of resolving family problems.

Authors' Preface

As I write this preface, I can't help remembering those dark and dreadful days immediately following my own separation. I had been married for twenty-two years and had four children. I was a respected and successful college professor and author. Then, with little warning, disaster struck. I found myself forced out of the house that had been my home for fifteen years. I was excluded from the lives of my children and separated from my familiar surroundings and the things I held dear. I had nowhere to turn. I was totally discounted. No one seemed to be aware of the depth of my pain.

I became embroiled in a vicious, uncaring and unfair adversary system. I was shocked and unprepared for the treatment I received from the legal system. The inhumanity I personally experienced at the hands of attorneys and judges sensitized me to the problems of others. I soon found that my situation was not unique, but was indicative of a national crisis. Society is using the wrong tools to solve delicate and emotional family-law problems. The American family-law system is wreaking havoc in the lives of fathers, mothers, grandparents, aunts, uncles, and, most important, children.

Today my life is back in order. I have married

a lovely lady who has taught me that the right partner can be the greatest asset a man can have. My wife Myrna has been of indescribable emotional assistance and support. She exhibited understanding and patience during the most difficult period of my life.

Americans are becoming unhappy with adversary divorce proceedings and the practice of awarding custody of minor children almost exclusively to women. There are changes in the wind. Millions of men are no longer willing to allow their children to be taken from them after divorce. They are fighting to remain fathers and asking for equal treatment in the courts. Men and women are joining hands in challenging archaic stereotypes that no longer hold true. Men are beginning to admit their need and ability to love, care for and nurture their children. It will be a grand day when we place the same importance on fathering as we do on mothering.

An increasing number of men and women are rejecting the courts in favor of conciliation, mediation and arbitration. There is a growing cadre of trained mental-health professionals whose services are being used to great advantage by divorcing spouses.

It is time we stopped producing wounded and injured victims in our family-law courtrooms and put our energy into stopping the war.

—*Gerald A. Silver*

When Jerry and I met I was in the throes of the most incredibly painful experience of my life. I had been married for twenty-three years and had two lovely daughters. The end of my marriage came suddenly and without warning. I was totally devastated. I had been a traditional housewife and felt unable to cope with the world alone after my separation. I thought my life was over. It was several months before I was willing to venture out of the house.

Shortly thereafter I met Jerry. While neither of us was emotionally whole enough to be able to fall in love yet, we developed a deep friendship and caring for one another. We gave each other support and understanding.

I soon realized that while I was receiving a great deal of sympathy and compassion from my friends and family, Jerry was almost totally alone. Men are frequently discounted by their friends and family after divorce. Few people seem to be aware of or moved by their suffering. Fortunately, Jerry's oldest son Steve exhibited a remarkable amount of sensitivity and maturity and was a source of comfort to him.

When I started attending meetings of the fathers'-rights group in which Jerry was involved, it became clear to me that many men were experiencing the same treatment that Jerry had encountered. I found a great rage growing in me at the attitude men have toward themselves. They discount their own worth as fathers and human beings. This marked the beginning of my involvement in the men's-rights movement. While I have become an ardent feminist, I feel I can be of more help in the cause of fathers' and men's rights. Women have gained the sympathy and help of men and women all over the country in their struggle for equality. But people still smile disparagingly when we talk about equality for men.

Jerry and I have become involved in each other's families and careers. In the middle of my life I have found myself possessing skills and talents I never dreamed I had. I have been given a second chance at life. We write, travel, and are involved in social reform. My days are interesting, exciting and fulfilling.

I have learned that gentleness, sensitivity, caring, love, and the ability to parent knows no gender. If I can help others understand this, perhaps it will result in bringing order out of the chaos in the lives of people enduring the trauma of divorce.

—Myrna Silver

Men's Rights and Divorce in the 1980's

1

We are their last resort. They come to us in desperation, not knowing where to turn. It usually begins with a phone call, sometimes in the middle of the night. They are unaware of the time. The pain is apparent in their voices. "Can you help me? My wife is taking my little girl away." We have to tell them there is no help—yet.

These are the "ex-fathers" by judicial decree. They come to us fresh from the courtroom, stunned by what they have just experienced at the hands of our legal system. "How can this be happening to me?" they ask. "I'm their father. They have no right. . . ."

But "they" do have a right. "They" are all-powerful. "They" are the robed monks who sit on the benches of our courtrooms and dispense "justice." "They" speak in an esoteric language about "OSC's," "declarations," "interrogatories" and "contempt." Before the legalistic ritual is over many men know the meaning of "contempt."

We have worked with innumerable fathers who are passing through the painful process of divorce. This book is based upon the knowledge gained from hundreds of men who have attended meetings, called us, written us, and come to our men's-rights group for help. We have also dealt with and been contacted by countless second wives, grandparents, attorneys, psychologists, social workers and others, whose experiences we have drawn upon for this book.

Perhaps you or someone close to you has been deeply affected by divorce and the dreadful emotional crisis that goes with it. Since experts tell us that nearly half of today's marriages will end in divorce, thousands of men, women and children are affected every day.

Their first contact with the inequities of the divorce system has forced many men to take a close look at their roles as males and fathers, their legal rights and emotional needs.

Very often the person who suffers the most pain and deprivation in the divorce process is the man. He not only experiences the trauma and heartache of losing his mate, he almost always loses his home and his children as well.

In these pages we are going to look at divorce and the breaking and restructuring of the family in the 1980's from the male point of view. We will also explore the new sensitivity males are developing toward themselves as human beings.

There is a revolution going on that is shaking the structure of our divorce system. Men are no longer content to quietly leave the house that has been home to them for many years. They are no longer content to become Weekend Fathers or ex-parents by judicial decree. They are no longer content to be mere money machines. They are banding together to protect their rights. Along with them are their new wives and their parents, who have suffered the pain of having their grandchildren excluded from their lives because they are on the "losing" side.

Millions of people subjected to the American system of divorce experience trauma, frustration and pain in an anachronistic court system that no longer meets their needs.

Many of the problems that are created by a divorce are unrecognized by society. We cannot settle these problems until we accept that divorce, child custody, child support and alimony difficulties are complex problems which cannot be solved by a single person or a stroke of a legislator's pen. Nothing short of a massive transformation in attitudes on the part of judges, attorneys and the public is needed to bring about significant change. Heartbreak and sometimes even suicide are the penalties we pay for the insensitivity society has displayed toward men.

Women find sympathy wherever they turn. Men are treated as if they have no feelings, almost as if they are invisible.

Before we go any further, lest our readers feel that divorce is fraught with only hopelessness and despair, let us tell you of some of the positive aspects. Many people find that their costly and painful divorce has turned out to be the best thing that ever happened to them. They are forced to look at themselves through new eyes and for the first time in their lives they like what they see. They go on to find greater happiness with a new mate or contentment in a new lifestyle as a single person. Life sometimes provides happy endings.

To illustrate, we were both married for over twenty years to other mates. Neither was the moving party in seeking divorce. There was long, protracted, very expensive litigation. Property settlements, alimony, child custody and support, contempt charges, forced sale of property, you name it—if one of us didn't experience it, the other did.

The divorce squabbles seemed to go on interminably, but they did finally end. Our lives had been shattered like pieces of fine china. However, instead of trying to put all the pieces back exactly the way they were before, we tried, successfully, to identify the best elements of our previous lives. Together we have constructed a new and even better relationship.

Women's Rights and Men's Needs

During the last several decades society has heard the cries of women. Feminists complain they are overworked, underpaid, shortchanged in the workplace, and have been dominated and exploited by husbands, fathers, sons, employers, the media, and even other women. Much of this is true and badly needed reforms have been instituted. Who today would seriously challenge equal pay for equal work or the right of a female to compete equally with males?

A proliferation of new laws, government agencies, self-help women's groups and a deluge of books, periodicals and magazines have addressed women's problems—and rightly so. But in this stampede to help women, men are being trampled.

The fight to treat the male equally in divorce matters is the first crack in the dike. Men are beginning to realize that they have also experienced significant discrimination in the criminal courts, the military and the workplace. Men are asking that women go to the front lines, be given equal sentences for criminal offenses, and that the plight of the battered husband be recognized. Men are rejecting the premise that as a group they are oppressing women, but rather that *they* are oppressed economically, socially and emotionally. Men are becoming cognizant of the real power in relationships—that it has often been the male, by virtue of his sex drive, who has been exploited and manipulated by the female. The truth is that both sexes have been subjugated by our cultural mores and stereotypes and by the media which have perpetuated them.

The absence of legislation and federal programs to help fathers and men is shameful. Perhaps worse are the one-sided and well-meaning efforts of district attorneys, judges and lawyers to protect primarily women. Men who fail to pay child support are ruthlessly tracked down by federal computer bloodhounds. Women who withhold visitation are not pursued at all. A woman who is beaten by her husband will receive aid and support, and then be directed to a federally funded center for victims of physical abuse. A man who is battered by his wife is laughed out of the police station.

For every male who is exploited or taken advantage of there is a second wife, sweetheart, parent or other close relative who is also hurting. Across the country there is a growing wave of resentment. In virtually every state in this nation there are increasing numbers of people bonding together to force change on a woefully outdated system. These groups, and films like "Kramer vs. Kramer," have raised the consciousness of many people who heretofore would have sat quietly by and taken it on the chin.

Fathers are going to court and demanding custody and the right to remain parents after divorce. They are beginning to demand equality in property settlements. Men are no longer willing to accept a second trust deed while their ex-wives take the house and everything in it. Men are refusing to pay alimony to educated, highly capable ex-wives. They are demanding that equal amounts of money be spent to solve male-related social problems. In short, men are buying the premise that equal really means equal.

What Statistics Don't Tell Us

Short of the rising crime rate, no subject has been studied, analyzed and dissected more than divorce. There is a mountain of information on family disintegration, the divorce rate, separations and desertions. Experts will give you the numbers on how many men don't pay child support. They can also tell you how many wives have been abandoned when they are past forty, so the husband can "do his thing" with a twenty-year-old. These statistics usually lead to a discussion about how impoverished the poor ex-wives and kids are, while Dad lives it up at the Marina.

What the statisticians don't report is the number of unhappy and heartbroken men who are sitting alone in a furnished room somewhere with nothing from the past but their clothing. Often they become depressed and view life as hopeless. While the statistics show that women attempt suicide more often than men, the reality is that three times as many males succeed in killing themselves each year.

The statistics don't talk of the poverty level many men are subjected to after paying exorbitant alimony and child support so the kids "won't have to have their lives disrupted." The experts ignore the statistics on how many homes, automobiles and bank accounts went to Mom for "the kids' sake." Many men are embittered by this experience and fear getting involved again. The numbers don't tell about the millions of dollars spent on courtroom battles provoked by fee-building attorneys. Statisticians are able to quantify how deprived and exploited women are, but they haven't reduced the abuse inflicted on men to numbers yet.

Let's take a look at some of the available data. The marriage rate has held relatively constant since the early 1900's. Approximately ten people per thousand are married each year. In 1978 there were 2,243,000 couples married. However, in 1978 there were also 1,122,000 divorces. While all marriages begin with the best intentions, nearly half of them are doomed to failure.

The reasons for the high divorce rate are manifold. Among the causes are social acceptance of divorce, women's liberation, and women's ability to be self-supporting.

Millions of children are affected by divorce. In 1955 only 347,000 children had divorced parents. By 1970 the number had grown to 870,000 and by 1977 there were 1,095,000 children living in broken homes. Thus the number of children of divorce has tripled in only two decades.

The number of children with mothers working outside the home has also shown a dramatic increase in the past several decades. In 1967 one out of every three kids had mothers actively engaged in the labor force. By 1978 it had escalated to one out of two. Now, besides having to adjust to a working mother, many kids have to deal with a broken home, often without a father.

A by-product of the rise in divorce and one-parent homes has been a substantial increase in juvenile delinquency. In 1960 there were over 25 million cases of juvenile delinquency handled by the courts. By 1976 the number had jumped to over 32 million cases. The incidence of juvenile delinquency has almost doubled in the last two decades. Further, child-neglect cases have also shown a considerable increase.

This kind of social disintegration and upheaval is not without its profit side. A growing army of lawyers and judges has been enlisted to staff our divorce courts. In 1972 there were 320,000 practicing lawyers and judges. By 1978 the number had grown to almost 500,000. A vast welfare bureaucracy has sprung up. The system supports a cadre of psychiatrists, counselors and social workers. It involves court clerks, probation officers and detectives in a massive social scheme to deal with the problems.

Each divorce, separation or child-custody battle leaves in its wake many frustrated, angry and unhappy human beings. Much of the burden has fallen upon the father who, over ninety-two percent of the time, is excluded from a close and loving relationship with his children after divorce.

Universal Themes

In our experience working with hundreds of fathers, their new wives, and other people whose lives touch theirs, there are certain common denominators. Let's go over some of the universal themes that crop up in almost every divorce.

Child custody. Undoubtedly the most anguishing and emotionally wrenching experience that divorcing couples go through is making provisions for the children. We take the position that there should be frequent and continuing contact with both parents after divorce.

This can best be accomplished through the awarding of joint physical and legal custody unless one of the parents is clearly incompetent. A major theme throughout this book will be the premise that fathers should not be excluded from the lives of their children, before or after divorce. The failure to recognize this keystone premise has created most of the heartache and problems in custody battles. In the chapters ahead we will look at various child-custody arrangements and how attitudes and opinions are changing.

Visitation. A high priority to millions of fathers is the subject of visitation. We take the position that the word "visitation" should be eliminated from the family-law vocabulary. One visits convicts in jail or patients in the hospital. One does not "visit" one's children. We believe that "co-parenting" or "shared custody" are more appropriate terms to describe an ongoing relationship between divorced parents and their children.

Child support. Much litigation and court time is spent dealing with child-support matters. We believe that the subjects of custody, visitation and child support are indivisible. The problems of child support will diminish when the father remains a part of the daily life of his children. We reject the heavy-handed approach by district attorneys who fail to provide equal administration of justice to both men and women in matters of child-support and visitation violations.

Property settlements. Short of child-custody and visitation matters, property settlements are the most hotly contested items in divorce. We support the premise that after divorce there should be a truly equal division of community property. We recognize that both partners contributed equally but differently to the marriage and that after divorce neither should benefit financially at the expense of the other. In these pages we will discuss the unfair treatment shown men by the courts when dealing with real estate, furniture or personal property acquired during the marriage. That is not to say that women do not also receive shabby treatment in these matters as well. But most often it is the men who end up with most of the nonliquid assets.

Alimony. In many states the term alimony has been replaced by the euphemism "spousal support." The words are different, but the meaning remains the same. With the growing number of women entering the labor force, the needs and aspirations of many of them are changing. We support the reasonable rehabilitation of a disadvantaged spouse. But we reject lifelong alimony payments which burden the male and force ex-wives to remain dependent on their former husbands. We encourage the premise that young women should take the attitude that men have traditionally taken. Women should seek maximum education and development of their personal abilities and remain contributing members of society.

Legal fees. The adversary system which chops partners apart with the brutality of a woodsman's axe is taken for granted and even defended by the legal profession, which profits the most from it. Couples who have reached an amicable settlement before they have seen an attorney are often pitted against each other by lawyers. The system seems to aggravate rather than conciliate litigants. In this book we will try to show you some alternatives. We believe that arbitration, mediation and conciliation are better means of reaching a settlement than the adversary process.

Our View of the Male

We believe that in this age there should be no fixed, unbending, straitjacketing roles for either the male or female partner. We reject the premise that housework and child rearing are "women's work" or that earning a living is exclusively the male's domain. That only women can feel pain and cry. That only mothers are nurturing parents and Dad's role is simply to discipline.

We accept the idea that people are individuals. We believe that most males do not recognize their disadvantaged positions. That many men fail to accept their inner feelings and that they fail to communicate and share these with other people. We believe in the full equality of both sexes and that everyone has a right to choose the role he or she will play, free from social pressure and stereotypes. We do not feel that men should carry a burden of guilt for having oppressed women, nor should they be willing to serve as "token males" or second-class citizens in the feminist movement.

We know there will always be those people who prefer to keep the traditional roles intact, and it is not our intent to force them into our mold. We simply want the freedom of choice.

We do not support a unisex society or the attenuation of differences between men and women. We believe men should lead the fight for equality of all human beings. It is a fallacy to believe that the feminist movement alone will bring equality to men. Much of the feminist rhetoric is focused on raising women to a point of superiority rather than equality.

How This Book Will Help You

We hope to give you some useful ideas and tools to help you deal with some of the most devastating problems you will ever face in your life, the problems of divorce. We will help you find your way through a maze of emotional, psychological, financial and legal troubles. We will show how you can continue to be a father and a man and yet not be a husband. We will help second wives understand their husbands' problems and talk about some of the difficulties faced by grandparents.

We define various custody arrangements and give examples of how couples have worked out day-to-day routines. We will help you recognize and deal with the games children play in divorce situations.

The chapter on attorneys will help you select and work with your lawyer. We will describe ways to conduct your divorce strategy in a manner that will create the fewest problems for yourself and your family. We will describe what to expect from the legal system and how to protect yourself. Hopefully when you finish this book you will be better prepared to identify and handle your problems.

Some Facts About the Fictions

2

"I want my freedom. I need some space and time to find myself." These words were still ringing in Richard's ears as he checked into the motel. His wife had been in therapy for the last few years and little by little things had been getting worse between them. They had been married for fourteen years and the decision to separate had not come easily. But Carol felt the need to strike out on her own. Now it was 2:00 A.M. and Richard found himself unable to sleep. The shock was beginning to wear off. He would have to find an apartment because the motel was expensive. He would need furniture, pots and pans, a toaster and God knows what else. "Maybe if I'm nice to Carol she'll let me borrow some dishes and linens until I can buy my own."

This story is played and replayed countless times in the lives of divorced men. It is interesting that when a woman leaves her home it is almost always her free choice. But when the couple decides to split up and the woman chooses to stay in the family home, the man has no choice at all. It is taken for granted that he will leave.

While many of our social values and customs are being questioned and changed, our view of men's emotions, needs and feelings has remained static.

To understand the American male of the 1980's, we must take a close look at the fictions and misconceptions that are deeply ingrained in our thinking. In this chapter we shall challenge some of the most prevalent ideas about men and their feelings. We will deal with how men respond to the effects of divorce and separation from their homes and families.

The Involuntary Exit

The exit of one partner from the family household is a critical event. It tends to establish a precedent or model that has deep financial and emotional repercussions. It should not be taken lightly. We believe that the partner who desires to leave the relationship should voluntarily leave the family dwelling. Presently, even if it is the woman who wants out of the relationship, it is rare for her to be expected to leave the home.

In our dealings with hundreds of men who have left their homes involuntarily we see a domino effect. Once they are ordered from the household the wife may ask for the house, the furniture, child support and usually alimony. We feel it is better for children to have both parents on an equal footing, even if their living arrangements are less luxurious, than have one parent enjoying the spoils of war.

The legal system reinforces many of our social biases. The Order to Show Cause proceeding is one of the most widely abused aspects of family law. It allows the male to be ejected from his household on the basis of unsubstantiated allegations. Judges will routinely dispossess a man from his home at the request of the wife. This is done because predominantly male judges have bought the old stereotype about men. The emphasis is upon protecting the "weaker sex" and it is taken for granted the man's needs are of less value.

Some men leave voluntarily because they share the same misconceptions about themselves. These men are not running away. They leave because of a desire to preserve the home for their children.

Men Are Vulnerable, Too

Our culture has brainwashed its males to hide their real feelings, not only from the world but from themselves. Men are taught from childhood to keep a stiff upper lip and deny what is going on inside.

We place unrealistic burdens and expectations on the man. When he cannot live up to these expectations, he develops a sense of failure and frustration. We expect our males to be all-American fathers, good performers in bed, fearless in the face of danger, and good providers. As boys grow older, these stereotypes are reinforced by their peers, teachers and, of course, by females. By the time our sons reach marriageable age, movies, television and the media have thoroughly instilled the John Wayne image into their consciousness. Men refuse to admit to themselves that they are limited in their abilities, sometimes inadequate, and in the end only human.

On the surface many males appear to manage separation from home and family, illness, and other upsets more easily than females. Many men find little support during times of trouble. Yet inside they are vulnerable and need as much protection and support as women in times of crisis.

It is interesting to see how males handle the dichotomy between their internal and external worlds. They laugh to the outside world while they are hurting inside. They lie to themselves and deny the reality of pain and loneliness. After divorce they sleep with as many women as they can to bolster their egos and alleviate their insecurities.

Some men place themselves on an endless social merry-go-round. They use an interminable string of parties, ski weekends and one-night stands to live up to the stereotype of the "free" man. Some men go into deep seclusion. They avoid friends and company. Their apartments become a refuge, piled high with dirty dishes, unemptied ashtrays, empty bottles and three-months' worth of old newspapers.

Still other men throw themselves into their careers, working night and day. There are men who hit the bottle with a ferocity that would make W. C. Fields look like a teetotaler. Some men overcompensate by placing heavy demands on their families. They insist on knowing every detail about their kids' lives and become overinvolved. Or they may shut their children out of their lives. They destroy the pictures and mementos of their past lives hoping to stop the pain.

The Continued Need to Father

It is widely believed that most fathers do not want to be burdened with children after divorce. The myth is that men feel the need for freedom more than women. This assumption is largely based on the fact that an extremely small percentage of men seek custody of their children.

The reality is that fatherhood is as natural to men as motherhood is to women. Men have the same need to share love with an offspring, to teach, guide, cuddle and hold their children as women. This fact is often denied by the legal system and by men themselves. It is often the father who is his own worst enemy. He denies what he feels in favor of what society has conditioned him to think he *should* feel.

This denial is rooted in a man's relationship with his own father. As he grows into young manhood he stops hugging his father and starts shaking hands. When his own child is born he is sometimes excluded from the delivery room. While his children are growing up his "place" is at the office. He takes little part in the children's daily life and is given little chance to become close. This process finally culminates in his exclusion from the children's lives after a divorce.

In order to continue sharing any part of his youngster's life he must convince the world that he is capable of being a parent. Mothers do not face this challenge.

Why don't more fathers seek custody of their children? After divorce a man must convince himself that he is not only qualified, but that in fact his presence is vital to the child's well-being. Then he has to convince his family—his parents, brothers and sisters, and even the children—of his continued need and right to father. Since he is flying in the face of established tradition, this is a monumental task in itself.

He is continually forced to prove himself as a man and a father.

If he should manage to succeed, he now has to convince his attorney, who rarely understands or sympathizes with his needs, and who usually is not on his side. Most attorneys do not question even the most derelict mother's right to custody. Indeed, they take her rights for granted. But they routinely challenge most men.

If the father should prevail with his family and his attorney, he then faces the most formidable obstacle of all—the judge. Steeped in the tradition of motherhood, most judges adamantly refuse to see men in any but the most conventional role. Is it any wonder then that so few men are willing or able to beat their heads against this wall of resistance?

Financial Abandonment

One almost doesn't question the notion that many fathers financially abandon their children after divorce. The myth of the high-living father who leaves his ex-wife and children to fend for themselves has been perpetuated, too often without substance. In fact, it has always amazed us how many men continue to pay child support and even alimony in the face of abuse and consistent disregard for their rights and feelings. Certainly there are fathers who don't pay for or visit their children after divorce. Many of these men neglected their families during the marriage also. There are many women, too, who deny their responsibilities both during and after the marriage. The real issue here is not how to deal with neglectful fathers, but rather neglectful parents. It is grossly unfair to place the onus of child neglect solely on men. All fathers should not be tarred with this brush.

A more subtle and elusive question is why loving and caring parents, fathers included, who are financially able, do not continue to underwrite their children's well-being after divorce. The answer lies in some insidious nuances of language and custom that too often go unnoticed. For instance, we hear a woman say, "I have little money for my kids while my 'ex' drives around in a Mercedes." Notice the use of the word "my" in the statement. Suddenly the kids are no longer "ours" but rather "mine." This attitude has driven many fathers from their children and dried up much of the financial support.

Almost without exception, when we look at the conditions under which child-custody arrangements were initially made, we find that the male was stripped of his children by judicial decree or social pressure. The root causes of the failure to provide are found in the deep hostility and resentment men feel at this disenfranchisement.

It is emotionally difficult, sometimes impossible, for some men to pay child support or visit their children at a home that they themselves paid for and later lost. For these men the pain of knocking on that front door like a stranger is so great, they can't handle it.

Men whose visitation rights have been consistently abused, or whose ex-wives have used the children as weapons against them, have taken a more extreme position. They cry, "no see, no pay," hoping that the only real lever they have — money — will help them see their children.

The fact that the father is cut off from seeing his children carries little or no weight with the law. Frequently the mother has the right to take the kids anywhere she chooses without informing the father when or if she is leaving or where she is taking them. Many judges allow a mother to take "her" children to another state or even another country.

A man who is sending his child-support check to a post office box, or who hasn't seen his children in several years, can hardly be faulted for less-than-enthusiastic compliance with court orders.

Single-Parent Households

The high rate of divorce has produced a number of single-parent households. We prefer to use the term "households," rather than single-parent "families." Single-parent households are sometimes unavoidable due to death, extended absence, or unwillingness of one parent to take responsibility. Where there does exist two loving, responsible parents, the courts should not shut one of them out.

It is difficult for one parent, no matter how loving and caring, to provide for the full needs of the children. It is hard enough for two parents, sharing responsibilities and contributing different but equal resources, to nurture a child.

Today many people advocate single-parent households, usually headed by women. There are a growing number of newspapers, organizations and groups which are aimed at supporting and giving legitimacy to single-parent households. The trend toward collective households, where several women band together to share responsibilities, does a serious disservice to the children. Putting more women in the house doesn't replace a man's influence.

Most studies show that children need access, modeling and role identification from both male and female. Households where there is only one parent tend to produce children who lack discipline and long-range goals, and who have problems of sexual identity. Little girls raised without a father may lack feelings of self-worth and self-esteem. They may view all males in a negative or adversary role.

Any probation officer or school principal can tell you that the most troubled children tend to come from homes where there is no father. When divorce is inevitable, we must find ways of making sure that the children are not deprived of one of their parents.

The Truth About Motherhood

There is a widespread belief that all women are naturally maternal and are instinctively capable of mothering and nurturing. It is assumed that most men are not interested in or capable of providing nurturing.

Nothing could be further from the truth. Many women deeply resent children in their lives. This is often covered up because of guilt, shame and fear of their own feelings. The disparity between what they are taught and their inner feelings is the basis for much of women's problems today.

Some mothers are willing to sell out the best interests of the children to buy their loyalty. The mother who allows—even encourages—a reckless teenager to take the family car against Dad's wishes is not really acting in the child's best interests. She is more concerned with her own need to keep the child on her side than with what is best for him.

Women are conditioned to take time off from pursuing their careers to raise a family. No one expects this from men. Women are forced into a mold that many resent. The Court, by almost always awarding sole custody to the mother, is reinforcing this concept.

The same judicial cookie cutter is at work on men. It is supposed that most men desire a full-time career with the role of father being secondary or incidental. The myth says that men do not want to be full-time fathers or play a nurturing role with their children. The truth is that many males desire close physical and emotional ties with their children. Many men want to play equal parts in bringing their children into adulthood. There is evidence of this everywhere we look. The father with a baby strapped to his back, the toddler in tow at the zoo, Junior racing Dad on the jogging path, or sitting on his lap at the office, all illustrate the nurturing instinct found in men. Yet society fails to acknowledge this.

Recently a successful young city attorney, at the height of his career, announced that he would not seek reelection. He explained to the press and the television cameras that time with his family was more important than reaching for another political goal. He plans to resume his career when his children are grown. It is interesting that this was considered front-page news. How many women make the front pages when they give up their careers to raise a family?

Children of Tender Years Stay with Mother

No single doctrine or premise has had a more negative impact on men than the assumption that very young children belong with Mother. In fact, children were awarded to father in contested-custody situations until the 1920's, when several significant court cases were handed down which had marked influence on child-custody orders. These established as though it were fact that nothing could substitute for a mother's love. Mother-love became equated with "the atmosphere of heaven." Thereafter judges routinely awarded exclusive custody to mothers regardless of the needs of the children.

We challenge this doctrine which for so many years has given women supremacy in the courtroom. What children of tender years need is years of tender care. The gender of the parent providing this care is immaterial. Tender loving care is provided by tender loving people. There is nothing inherent in the makeup of the woman which makes her superior to the man in this respect.

A case can be made that infants who are nursing should remain with Mother for biological reasons. However, nursing only lasts for a few months. The warmth, cuddling and closeness that gives the baby a feeling of love and security can be provided by both sexes.

Children Don't Always Know Best

We often assume that children instinctively make choices that are in their best interests. One dietician said that if left alone to choose, children automatically picked a balanced diet. Any parent with teenagers recognizes that burritos, soda pop and french fries do not fit that description.

Children intuitively choose that course of action which allows them the most freedom and the most immediate gratification of short-term needs. This is evident in many divorce and custody situations where children opt to go with Mother. In many instances the father is looked on as the heavy because he is the one who sets the rules and administers discipline.

Judges often question youngsters as to which parent they would like to live with. It is natural for the children to select the more lenient and generous parent in these circumstances. Some insightful psychologists are now saying that we should place less emphasis on the child's preferences. Children do not have the wisdom and maturity to appreciate that the parent who says "no" is often showing more care and love than the one who takes the line of least resistance and says "yes" without considering all the consequences.

Frequently the child's decision is also swayed because staying with Mother usually means he doesn't have to leave his familiar surroundings. Thus the territorial imperative is at work here and many times overrides any other consideration. The child may be opting for the place, not the person.

Who Holds the Power

It is assumed that the disposition of the family home, furniture and other assets is in the hands of professionals and reasonable adults. Judges and (indirectly) attorneys, and to a lesser extent the litigants themselves, wield much influence. The truth is, however, that where the children go, so goes the property. This gives the children a great deal of power. Older children in particular may be quite sensitive to this.

A child who opts to go with Mother because she throws more goodies in the pot has the power to see that she gets the house. The progression is as follows, and might properly be referred to as the Divorce-Domino Theory: Mom gets the kids, and of course the pets stay with them too. Since she has the family, she needs the house. One can't have a house without furniture, and Dad has no place to put it anyway, so it goes to Mom. Now she must pay for all this; ergo, large child-support and alimony payments. And so the dominoes fall, one after another.

No-Fault Divorce Is No Cure-All

It has been widely assumed that no-fault divorce has eliminated much of the bitterness and hostility in divorce actions. To the uninitiated it may appear that states with no-fault divorce laws have reduced acrimony and expenses and have made the divorce process less painful. Certainly no-fault divorce has brought a new vocabulary. We now find "respondents" instead of "defendants," "divorce" has become "dissolution," and "alimony" is now called

"spousal support." These labels are only cos-
metic changes, however; no-fault divorce is not
an adequate solution to the real problem.

The courtroom continues to be a war zone
and a place to vent hostile feelings and retali-
ate against one's spouse. Before no-fault, couples spent a lot of money on lawyers, professional services and litigation. After no-fault
they are still spending a lot of money on lawyers, professional services and litigation. No-
fault requires an equal division of community
property without the placement of blame. Now
accountants, appraisers, auditors, psychiatrists
and social workers are the hired guns. Horren-
dous battles are raged over custody, property
settlements, evaluations of businesses and alimony awards. Litigants still punish each other
through the adversary process. Later we will
discuss some better alternatives to the present
system.

The Family-Law Courts

Discovering the true nature of the divorce
courts is probably the biggest shock experienced by litigants. After watching judges and
attorneys on television for many years, we get
a rude awakening in the real courtroom. Both
men and women are dismayed to find that
there is pitifully little justice and fairness to be
found. There are no Perry Masons or Owen

Marshalls out there. The callous attorneys and the biased judge as portrayed in "Kramer vs. Kramer" are more like the reality.

Many divorce attorneys handle a high volume of cases, with the clock running at from $75 to $125 per hour. Some attorneys have specialized in high-priced "Hollywood" divorces. They have obtained enormous property settlements. These expensive attorneys prepare their cases with great diligence, rely upon expert witnesses, and use every resource available.

But the average person who hires an attorney finds a very different standard. Many attorneys spend a minimum of time preparing their cases. They review a file in the hall shortly before a hearing, fail to prepare adequate declarations or points and authorities, and on occasion get their clients mixed up. Their fees are not contingent upon the quality of their performances. They opt for solutions that make their work easier and then blame their failures on the "system" or a "biased judge."

Expediency and convenience for judge and attorney are paramount over administration of justice. Our courts are full of untrained and insensitive judges. There is virtually no monitoring or reporting of either attorneys' or judges' performances.

Courts routinely lose or misplace files. There is no security system to check on files taken out for review. There are bottles of correction fluid in the file room. Records of hearings are often incomplete or nonexistent.

Much important decision making is done in chambers with clients excluded from these discussions. Also excluded is the court reporter, and thus there is no appealable record. Attorneys do a lot of bargaining in chambers. The rules of evidence are suspended and judges make decisions based on information related by attorneys rather than information elicited through testimony. In one case we know of involving a twenty-year marriage, a family business, sizable property, and children, the judge called opposing counsel into chambers. The case had finally come before him after a number of postponements and several days of sitting in the hallway waiting for a courtroom. At last, at ten minutes to 4:00, the judge asked both counsel to state their cases in private. At 4:10 the judge made up his mind and informed the attorneys to tell their clients how he had decided to rule. If they accepted his ruling, fine. If they decided to present their case, then he would up the ante of the party who wanted to try the case. The client accepted the challenge, the case was tried, and the judge ruled exactly as he said he would, completely ignoring the evidence.

Perjury is rampant in the family-law courts. The rules of evidence that give one some measure of protection in the criminal courts are scarcely in evidence in divorce trials. A judge often will accept a declaration made by one spouse against the other at face value. He also may preclude vital records from evidence without foundation.

The family-law courts give wide discretionary power to judges. Judgments may be based on bias or prejudice, rather than on factual considerations. It is virtually impossible to overturn a verdict because of abuse of this discretion.

It is under these circumstances that the courts dispose of hundreds of cases each month with little regard for the long-range impact on the lives of those involved.

Reevaluation of the Male Role

3

In the 1940's we loaded ships and planes with men and sent them off to foreign shores to die in the name of freedom, equality and justice. The blood that was shed came from whites, blacks and other minorities. The common denominator was they were all men. When the survivors returned to the suburbs and ghettos of America, they were sensitized to the patent bias and prejudice all around them.

This new awareness led to the fight for equality that culminated in the Civil Rights Act of 1964. Blacks questioned and later successfully overthrew the customs which forced them into the back of the bus and disenfranchised them as human beings. Society began to seriously question its rules, treatment and attitudes toward minorities. The first step in correcting any social injustice is the recognition of its existence.

The feminist movement gained much impetus from the Civil Rights Act. Angry housewives in the early 70's marched waving placards and johnny-mops, demanding release from their slavery. Some of the strongest supporters of the feminist movement were men who were deeply disturbed by the inequities they saw. Affirmative-action plans, equal-opportunity programs and Justice Department suits attest to how society is aggressively moving to identify and solve problems related to women.

Our Social Blind Spot

There is one area of myopia in all this clamor for equality. Society has not turned its spotlight of awareness on male inequities with the same intensity it has focused on women. A handful of men are beginning to wake up to the fact that they are a major oppressed minority.

The average American male today does not raise an eyebrow when women sit around in consciousness-raising sessions. The same man will be shocked at the suggestion that he lacks a consciousness of his own problems. Most men are blind to the discrimination and unrealistic expectations they encounter every day.

There is no strong organized national movement of men or women seeking to define the rights of males and correct the inequities. Later we will talk about some of the emerging coalitions—groups of fathers, second wives and grandparents—that are becoming sensitive to men's rights. At this time there is no national sentiment or recognition of the seriousness of the problem. If we are going to be a truly equal society, the next major revolution must be men's rights.

Let us now explore the etiology of the male dilemma and the social pressures at work on men both from within and without.

Our attitudes are principally a product of our early family life. From infancy we gain an appreciation of who and what we are from those closest to us. Our mothers and fathers are primary influences, teaching us how to behave and defining what is expected from us. Later our brothers and sisters begin to refine and further shape our roles.

When we start school peer influences become very important. By the time we reach puberty our perceptions of ourselves are well fixed. These are confirmed throughout our lives by television, motion pictures and other media.

The process is ongoing. The male's selection of and success in a career are extremely important in the eyes of the world. Many a man has endured a lifetime spent in a career he really doesn't enjoy. But since a man is judged by what he does, some men trade off emotional fulfillment for prestige and monetary rewards.

Thus our careers, family relations and peer groups tell us what we are expected to be. Here are some ways we see ourselves:

Males are:	*Females are:*
strong	soft
aggressive	passive
unemotional	easily moved
breadwinners	homemakers
disciplinarians	caring, nurturing
insensitive	feeling
stoic	communicative

and so the list goes on. . . Females are seen to be warm, caring, nurturing people, while men are seen as providers of protection and material goods. Our natural cultural bias is fostered subliminally and overtly in many ways.

A visitor from outer space seeking the most descriptive artifact of our modern culture would be hard pressed to find a more useful document than the "Sears 1980 Spring/Summer Catalog." What would his impression be of our society upon examining this item? He would see that there are various types of Earth people and that they come in different colors. They come in two categories, male and female, with clearly defined roles.

Women are nurturers of children (many pictures of women holding babies, p. 378). Women dress not only the kids but their men as well (pp. 446 and 469). Little boys ride mini-bikes and mopeds (p. 646). Little girls cuddle dolls (p. 364). Men paint autos (p. 772) and houses (p. 773). Women care for pets (pp. 780 and 782), do the vacuuming (p. 1054) and wash the clothes (p. 1046). Men cook, but only on outdoor barbecues (p. 1080). Women file papers (p. 1194) and men are the architects and builders (p. 1198).

Would this alien visitor conclude that little boys have cuddling instincts or that some little girls prefer a rambunctious ride on a mini-bike? Would he conclude that some of our women would like to be painters, builders and planners, or that some males would love a chance to be domestic?

This type of reinforcement of role models bombards us wherever we turn, every day of our lives. What does this do to the male? It makes him feel uncomfortable admitting that he enjoys holding the baby, dressing the kids or avoiding heavy physical work. He may love to cook. If he does, he'd better be sure his cooking is a "hobby" or he will be considered unmanly.

Even our language reinforces the stereotypes. Does anyone question the meaning of "strong, silent type," "he-man," or "act like a man"? Just as clear are the meanings of "woman's work" and "woman's prerogative." When a woman is discussed in the media she is described as a wife and mother, while a man is characterized by his occupation or profession.

A man is expected to feel fulfilled by his career or his work just as in the past women were supposed to be satisfied with being housewives and mothers. Women are now admitting that they need more, but men have not yet advanced to this point of enlightenment. Many men, having been forced to neglect their families in order to further their careers, find that work is no substitute for family.

The Price Men Pay

All of these inequities have taken a heavy emotional and physical toll on the American male in the twentieth century. The price men pay is nowhere more clearly illustrated than in an examination of the life expectancy differences between men and women. In 1920, women outlived men by an average of one year. By 1977, women were living almost eight years longer. Substantially more men than women die each year of heart disease, pneumonia and cirrhosis of the liver. Men are almost two-and-a-half times more prone to die violently because of accidents and homicides.

Though much has been written about the physical price men pay, little attention has been paid to the emotional consequences of a lifetime spent trying to live up to their collective self-image.

Today's male is afraid to really look at himself for fear of what he will find. If he doesn't admit certain things, perhaps he will not have to do anything about them. However, if he takes a good look, an honest self-appraisal, this is what he will see: an overworked, underpaid, overrated, underestimated human being. Under the protective outer shell is a vulnerable and insecure person, not so different from his female counterpart after all.

For many years the male has had to be the all-knowing, all-providing and all-powerful rock of Gibraltar. If he crumbles under stress, his family and friends are shocked and dismayed. This has been a crushing emotional and psychological burden, from which death has sometimes been the only escape. Even divorce does not lift the burden and sometimes makes it worse.

For many males the growth of the feminist movement has promised some relief from this enormous responsibility. Finally, after all these years, some women are willing to pick up their share of the load. Some men see the ERA as the removal of women from the "protected-species" class. Others fear and fight the coming of the ERA. Much of their resistance is due to the inconsistency of feminist goals and the strident rhetoric and behavior of some of the women'srights leaders.

In theory there is little to reject in any movement which mandates equality. Many feminist ERA advocates call for full equality of both sexes. They expect to stand and die beside the men on the battlefield. They don't want to be favored in the courts in matters of child support, custody and alimony. Taken to its fullest, ERA should mean fully equal treatment in the eyes of the law.

Unfortunately many feminist leaders are asking for conditional equality. They want promotions and pay raises, but they don't want to register for the draft. Feminist Karen Seal in an article written for *Family Advocate*, a national legal journal, called for a return to a system of unequal distribution of community property. She asked for a rewriting of California law to give women preferential treatment with respect to distribution of assets and alimony. She even suggested that wives receive the family home simply on the basis of their feminine status.

Many more men would support the ERA if its supporters took a position of unconditional equality. Women should expect not only equal pay for equal work, but to work as fire fighters, coal miners and as members of SWAT teams. Equal numbers of men and women must be prepared to pay the price for living in and defending society and our way of life.

Women should be given equal jail terms and fines when they commit crimes. At present women generally receive lighter sentences than men. In 1977 there were over 267,000 males in federal and state prisons. By contrast, there were only a little over 11,000 females in jail. Thus police, district attorneys, judges and juries have put twenty-six times as many males behind bars as females.

Is it any wonder that women like Phyllis Schlafly are fighting tooth and nail against ERA to keep the "perks" that women have enjoyed through the years? The reversals that the ERA has suffered thus far attest to the savvy many women are showing in going after only those areas of equality which bring the privileges without the responsibilities.

Many women who are holding good jobs, and who consider themselves "equal," will stand in front of a closed door waiting for a man to open it, will insist that their man order the meal and choose the wine in a restaurant and, of course, expect him to pay the bill. They call it "retaining their femininity." We call it "selective equality."

A Sexual One-Way Street

Virtually everyone recognizes the changing sexual morality of the female in the 1980's. But little is said about the effects of this new morality on men. Until recently sex roles were rather clearly defined. Men were expected to be aggressive and females passive. He was supposed to make advances and it was her prerogative to reject them. If the man did not make the expected pass, the female was insulted.

At parties and dances men were expected to approach women and were conditioned to accept rejection. If a girl didn't reject a pass, she was considered "loose." This placed everyone in a no-win situation.

Times have changed for the female. But many men have been unable to escape their previous conditioning. The 1980's woman has allowed herself the freedom to accept or reject sexual advances. She also feels free to be the one making the advances. She may look over the crop of males at the singles' bar, cut one out from the herd, and aggressively go after him. A woman can take a man home to bed and send him away the next morning with a free conscience, just as men have always been allowed to do.

Women have recognized their right to sexuality and are taking full advantage of it. This speaks well for the female's ability to accept and live with major social changes.

But men are having a great deal of trouble acclimatizing to this new way of life. Some men enjoy being the object of pursuit and have thrown themselves into this new morality with gusto. However, the majority of males are unable to accept it. Men have been so deeply conditioned to be the hunter that they cannot handle being the prey. They feel their masculinity is being threatened.

The 1980's male does not have the same support and acceptance to help him adjust to a new standard. He is not accustomed to being treated like the female of the 1950's. He does not have years of tradition behind him of being treated like a sex object. Many newly divorced males will tell you their most unnerving experience was the first time they were picked up by a female, used sexually, and sent on their way.

A lot of men resent aggressive women. They dislike the phone calls, the invitations to go to dinner or spend a weekend out of town. They want a "good old-fashioned woman" who "knows her place." These men are seeking an increasingly rare commodity, one which is becoming an endangered species.

Nancy Reaganism

She stands slightly behind him, perfectly dressed and coiffed, and smiles up at him as he speaks. She is the submissive little woman who looks adoringly up at her big, strong, wonderful husband. She lives for him and basks in his glory. Nancy Reagan is the epitome of this stereotype.

Tradition dictates that "a smart woman is not smarter than her husband." Many women feel compelled to play down their intellect and ability in order not to overshadow a sometimes ordinary male. There is some complex psychology at work here. Some women are afraid to tread on their husbands' egos. Others wish to avoid adult responsibility. Still others fear that they may not be able to harness their intelligence and capability once exposed.

Men also play the game. They accept this caste system because they too are afraid of the challenge to their egos and intellect.

Recently we went out to dinner with a couple in their mid-fifties who have been married for many years. When dinner arrived her soup was cold. Social convention dictated that her husband ask the waiter to have the soup heated. He did so. When the soup was brought back it was still lukewarm. The husband now felt compelled to make an issue of the event by calling the manager. After the matter was resolved, the hostility apparent at the table remained throughout the evening.

The man was resentful at being forced into acting as a buffer between his wife and the incompetent restaurant staff. Yet he would not allow his wife to speak for herself as this would interfere with his role as her protector. The wife confided later that she felt angry at not being considered competent to handle the situation herself. Thus, her concern for his ego and his regard for her fragility resulted in two frustrated, angry people.

Another example of the damage done by stereotypes that do not reflect reality is illustrated in the case of two educated, intelligent friends of ours. She had the higher IQ and ability to solve problems. However, social convention dictated that he be the intellectual leader in the household. She was forced to turn to him for answers to questions that she could solve better and faster. She had to use subterfuge to make him think that her ideas were his. Thus, once more, learned patterns of behavior won out over common sense. This couple ended up divorced some years later.

Few families have an intellectual surplus and the waste of this valuable resource is shameful. These patterns are observed and followed by the children in the family and as a consequence destructive role playing is perpetuated through the generations.

The failure to admit a partner's innate intellectual capabilities has sown the seeds of many a divorce. It is at the root of much of the unhappiness between couples.

Equal Responsibility

When a substantial number of men and women recognize the inequities, there will be many demands for change. For example, divorced men who are unemployed will demand alimony, just as women have done for years. Society will expect the same punishment or jail sentences to apply to both sexes. Women will serve in the front lines along with men during times of war. Joint legal and physical custody of children will be routinely granted. An equal division of community property will be the accepted order of things.

Both parents will be held equally responsible for the financial needs of their children. Roles that are not comfortable will not be forced on individuals. In the Sears catalog of the future, Father will be as free to rock the cradle as to drive the tractor, and Mother will be as much at home with a power saw as with a sewing machine.

Disneyland Dads

4

The aroma of roasting turkey permeated the air of Bill's small apartment. Bill's mom and dad had come from halfway across the country to spend Thanksgiving with Bill and their granddaughter, Lisa, whom they hadn't seen since the divorce two years ago. All the arrangements had been made. Bill had sent his ex-wife the money for Lisa's air fare and she would be arriving at the airport on the 1:30 flight.

Bill left early because he knew his nine-year-old would be frightened if the plane landed and Daddy weren't there. After battling his way through the traffic on the freeway and the jungle of the airport loop, Bill finally found a parking space in Lot C, about half a mile away. He arrived at the gate, breathless, in time to watch the holiday ritual.

As people started to disembark, he saw several stewardesses shepherding their small charges through the gate to waiting fathers. Bill was glad Lisa was finally old enough to take care of herself. He watched anxiously as two more children came through the gate and were snatched up by their waiting dads. There was lots of excited chatter and much hugging and kissing.

It soon became apparent that Lisa was not on this flight. Bill went aboard the plane in case she had fallen asleep, but she was nowhere in sight. A long-distance call told the whole story. "I decided not to send Lisa after all. My parents are coming for Thanksgiving and they want to see her. I'll send her next week." When Bill arrived back at his apartment, the disappointment and rage that he felt were reflected in the faces of his parents when he walked through the door alone.

This is life as a Disneyland Dad. There are a hundred variations of Bill's story acted out at airports across the country every holiday. The Disneyland Dads of this generation are the men, disenfranchised of their parental rights, who are forced to grovel in front of their ex-wives for a crumb of time with their children.

Men did not always have to play second fiddle to their former wives. The phenomenon of awarding sole custody to mothers is a product of recent times. In England, as late as the 1700's, the father's right to custody of the children was virtually unquestioned.

A gradual shift started in the early 1800's, when the famous poet Percy Shelley was refused custody because he was an atheist. Then in 1839 the courts were given discretion in some custody cases under Talfourd's Act. This act eroded the father's right to absolute custody by permitting awards to mothers of children under seven years of age. This opened the way for the "tender-years" doctrine which has survived to the present day. The pendulum had swung to a position of equality in England by 1925 when the Guardianship of Infants Act was passed.

In the United States, custody decisions followed the common law of England. In the 1800's fathers were considered better able than mothers to raise children. In fact, in an 1857 New York case a judge awarded a nursing child to the father. Later, in an 1860 New Hampshire case, the judge stated, "The father is entitled to the custody of his minor children as against the mother and everybody else." Up until the early 1900's mothers who did gain custody were not even entitled to any support from the father.

When did this start to change? Around the turn of the century, psychologists and behaviorists began to look at sex relationships and parenting. They found that the interests of the children were being overlooked. Soon a clear trend developed which made the welfare of the child paramount in decisions concerning children. Later this became known as the "best-interests-of-the-child" doctrine.

Courts began to grant custody on the basis of their perception of the child's best interests. It was supposed that the mother, being the one who breast-fed and nurtured the child, was a more fit parent than the father, who was away from home most of the day providing for the economic needs of the family. The pendulum swung farther and farther in favor of the mother as judges overreacted to the "best interests of the child." It reached the point where custody was being given to mothers ninety-two percent of the time.

That is not to say that fathers got custody the rest of the time. The other eight percent was divided among grandparents, other family members, non-relatives and fathers.

The final crushing blow came with the publication in 1973 of *Beyond the Best Interests of the Child*, by Joseph Goldstein, Albert Solnit and Anna Freud. This book gave professional validity to the concept that it was in the child's best interests to be given to one parent. Thus the courts in the 1970's were given a justification to exclude fathers from custody. The "beyond-the-best-interests" philosophy permeates family law and vindicates the biases of judges, attorneys, psychologists and district attorneys.

It is through the research of Judith Wallerstein, a fellow at the University of California at Berkeley, and other enlightened behaviorists, that the courts are beginning to see the need for close and continued contact of both parents with children after divorce. A handful of perceptive activists, dozens of men's-rights groups, and a pitifully small sprinkling of family-law professionals are starting a pull on the pendulum in the hope of bringing it to a middle ground.

Later in this book we will touch upon the growth of the men's-rights movement and how fathers are fighting to reverse the damage done by the "best-interests" philosophy. For now let us look at the harvest of Disneyland Dads that has been reaped as a result of this doctrine.

The Disenfranchised Father

A Disneyland Dad is a male who has lost custody, either by court decree or social custom, and who desires a relationship with his children but is frustrated by his ex-wife or the legal system. Further complicating the problems faced by these men are the power given to the custodial parent by the simple act of being given custody, and the brainwashing which ensues during the daily contact with the children.

The scenario that follows has been repeated a thousand times over by fathers who come seeking help from men's-rights groups. The story usually begins with the granting of a typical court order giving the father "reasonable" visitation rights, with physical custody granted to the mother. Many men do not fight this order at the time of the dissolution because it seems fair to them. It also seems more workable than a rigidly spelled-out set of rules or calendar dates.

They very quickly come to rue this decision, as it turns into a nightmare of endless litigation. The problem is caused by the interpretation of the word *reasonable*.

Relying upon reasonable visitation rights, Dad calls to take the kids out to dinner and a movie. At first Mom is quite amenable to letting the kids go when Dad calls. Soon, it becomes increasingly difficult for Dad to keep thinking up new ways of keeping the kids occupied. He usually has a small apartment where there are no other kids for them to play with. Children are not allowed at the pool and there is no fenced yard. So Dad takes them to the park, to the bowling alley, to the movies, to a baseball game and to Disneyland. It costs him a fortune, and the kids become restless and irritable. By the end of the day they are tired and want to go home. He delivers them to their mother, whining and cranky. It takes her two days to settle them down. Then for the next few days all she hears about is how much fun they had with Dad.

The following week he is a half-hour late because he was held up in traffic. Mom has had to deal with nagging, impatient children, besides being made late for an appointment of her own. The seeds of hostility are being sown in all concerned.

Dad is running out of places to take the kids.

He wants to be part of their everyday lives and not just see them in an unnatural environment. The kids are making more and more demands on both parents and are beginning to play one off against the other.

Mom is getting fed up with the whole thing. On the next visit, which has now become a chore, Dad has had to turn down an invitation to spend the weekend out of town with his new girlfriend because he doesn't want to disappoint the kids. He picks them up and off they go to the park. When he brings them home, the younger child is hysterical because she was scared by a big dog in the park and the older one has a stomachache because he ate three hot dogs, a jumbo helping of french fries, and two ice cream cones.

Next time Dad goes to pick up the children his ex-wife greets him at the door. He can see she is angry. She launches into a diatribe about his inconsideration, lack of concern for the kids, and irresponsibility. "From now on you'll see the kids when I say so and no other time!" And the door is slammed in his face. Her explanation to the kids is, "Dad doesn't want to see you today." The father stands looking at the closed door, thinking, "She can't do this. I have some rights." He is soon to find out otherwise.

Sometimes this withdrawal of visitation is done more subtly. Dad comes to the door only to be told that his child is in bed with the flu. Or Mom may schedule "important" appointments on days Dad is supposed to see the children.

There are different problems with older children. Teenagers prefer to spend their time with their peers. Since they live at home, this is not a problem for Mother. She's sure to see them at mealtimes. But Dad is cut out of their lives. They are too busy to see him.

Fathers tell us that the time they feel the most helpless and suffer the most pain is when their ex-wives move away with the children. In many states the custodial parent is allowed to take the children anywhere in the country. The only constraint in relocating a child to another jurisdiction is that it not affect the child's welfare. No consideration is given to the non-custodial parent's rights, feelings or desires.

A custodial parent may take a new job or remarry and move across the state or even across the country. Some have been known to move to a foreign country. The other parent is helpless to stop the move, even though it frustrates visitation.

So Disneyland Dads fly across the country, holing up in cheap apartments or motels and living out of suitcases, in hopes of spending a little time with their children. Some men can't handle the emotional distress or the financial hardship this causes them and give up trying to see their children entirely.

The law does not force a custodial parent to disclose the whereabouts of the children to the other parent. Thus there are men who are paying child support to post office boxes and haven't seen their children for years. Regardless of their wealth or their success in a new marriage and a new family, nothing fills the void caused by the loss of a child.

In our group we have show-business personalities, doctors, policemen, businesspeople, day laborers, and even a handful of lawyers. All are treated equally cavalierly by the family-law courts with respect to custody and visitation matters.

After having talked with hundreds of parents and corresponded with a great many more, it has become very clear that the link between being part of the lives of the children and paying for their support is a critical one. Many legislators and custodial parents deny this vehemently and claim there is no connection. In fact, some states have passed laws expressly stating that child support and visitation enforcement are unrelated. Yet the only leverage many men have to see their children is child support. Their battle cry is, "no see, no pay!"

The Tragedy of Child Stealing

A particularly distressing by-product of custody disputes is the increasing incidence of child snatching. Thousands of children are kidnapped annually by disgruntled and unhappy noncustodial parents. The figure is estimated to be as high as 100,000 per year. This causes untold emotional and psychological damage to the children and doesn't solve the problem.

In a typical child-stealing situation, a father's visitation rights have been grossly abused by the ex-wife. She may limit or frustrate visitation, or be planning to leave the jurisdiction. Some men think that their only alternative is to take the child, since the district attorney does not enforce their rights. These males live in fear of apprehension, change their identities, and move from town to town. This is the price they are willing to pay to be close to their children.

Sometimes the child stealing is perpetrated by women who feel the natural father should not see his children, regardless of the court order. In most situations, the underlying problem is that one parent has been excluded, while the other gains "property rights" over the children. In all cases, the children suffer the most.

Unequal Administration of Justice

Many men complain bitterly that there is unequal enforcement of the law. Some laws are stringently enforced while others are ignored. Nowhere is this bias more prevalent than in the area of family law.

The collection of child-support payments is vigorously enforced against men. In fact a national locator system has been implemented to chase down men who fail to meet their obligations. Yet the violation of visitation rights goes virtually unpunished by district attorneys and the courts. There is sound economics behind this unequal enforcement. By tracking down errant fathers, the County is able to cut down on its welfare costs.

California has a law on its books which makes it a crime to frustrate a noncustodial parent's visitation rights. Men who have been denied their rights have approached their local police departments with copies of the law and their court orders in hand. They are told, "This is a civil matter. Go talk to your attorney." When the district attorney is appealed to, the fathers are told, "We don't want to minimize your problem, but we don't have the staff or money to help you."

The district attorney's office is not encouraged to go after a woman who denies visitation, and will rarely do so. In this way, the Disneyland-Dad syndrome is sanctioned by the police department, the district attorney's office and the courts.

The Effects of Weekend Fathering

Society pays a heavy price to maintain its Weekend-Father structure. It is emotionally and psychologically bankrupting to all concerned. Dad becomes merely a money machine. His lot in life is to be the paying agent without the rewards and close relationship of a family. He is forced into an unnatural relationship with his children.

It is virtually impossible for the male to maintain authority, positive influence and control over his children in this environment. Finally, he must continually prove himself. To his children, he must prove that he is still their father. He must prove to his ex-wife that he is worthy of seeing his children, and he lives in fear of her wrath. Deep inside, he must prove to himself that he is still a man.

The Disneyland-Dad syndrome exacts a heavy toll on women as well. First and foremost they must deal with the burden of sole custody. The responsibility of children is awesome even when shared. When borne alone it sometimes becomes a crushing weight. Women experience a lack of freedom which affects their careers and social life. They frequently are unable to handle the demands of disciplining the children. They must hide their failure to control the kids in order to save face. The bad grades, traffic tickets and drug experimentation must be kept from Dad at all costs.

The highest price is frequently paid by the children. Research shows that children deprived of one parent grow up starved of a natural balance. They lack the role models and the security of knowing that they have two caring parents. This may affect their entire adult lives. In the next few chapters we will look at the father as a nurturing parent and we will explore alternatives to Disneyland fathering, including joint custody, co-parenting, and other mutual arrangements.

Life ———————————
Without
Father

5

The Census Bureau recently reported that the number of one-parent households jumped nearly eighty percent in the last decade. This means that almost one out of every five families with children is headed by one parent. According to the report, the percentage of one-parent families headed by divorced women climbed from twenty-nine percent to thirty-eight percent.

Numerous psychologists and researchers are scrutinizing the impact of excluding one parent from the life of the children. In this chapter we are going to take a close look at the psychological implications of fatherless households and their effects on mothers, fathers and children.

Judith S. Wallerstein, in the January 1980 issue of *Psychology Today*, discusses the results of her in-depth study of how children react to divorce. Wallerstein tracked children from bro-

ken families for five years. She found that
thirty-four percent of these children were
happy and thriving, twenty-nine percent were
doing reasonably well, and thirty-seven percent were depressed and unhappy.

The children who fared best were those who
had full and loving relationships with both father and mother. Wallerstein found it to be essential for fathers to maintain a continued
closeness to their children. She has become a
very strong advocate of continuing contact
with both parents for children of divorce.

Children who did not have a stable, loving relationship with both parents exhibited many
problems. Many children were intensely unhappy and dissatisfied after their parents split
up and felt guilty and responsible for the absence of the missing parent.

Over twenty-five percent of these children experienced extreme loneliness, even though one
parent was still there. Almost twenty-five percent felt anger, reflecting underlying fear, sorrow, and a sense of powerlessness. Temper
tantrums, delinquent behavior, drug abuse, and
stealing were also widely manifested in children from single-parent homes.

Some of the children expressed a great desire
to remain close to the father who was excluded
from the family. According to Wallerstein, one
youngster saved a dozen dog-eared, folded and
refolded letters and reread them frequently.
They had been sent to her by her father.

Among the most painful experiences for the

children were those situations where the
mother and stepfather demanded that the kids
renounce their love for their father as a price
for acceptance and affection. These children became severely troubled and depressed. Wallerstein concludes, "It seems clear that our society
must encourage fathers and mothers to accept
the importance of continuity in parent-child relationships after divorce."

Our own observations suggest that Wallerstein may be understating the case. Children of
divorce exhibit not only internal emotional
problems, but they manifest many external
antisocial-behavior patterns as well. For instance, we know a case of a couple with two
teenaged boys. After the father was excluded
from the home, and custody given to the
mother, the boys became directionless. The
younger boy dropped out of school. When the
father advised him that this was an unwise decision with far-reaching effects, the sixteen-
year-old exclaimed, "I don't have to do what
you say. You aren't my father anymore."

The eighteen-year-old boy began drinking,
which resulted in several drunk-driving convic-
tions. Many fathers describe similar experiences, where their lack of authority resulted in
serious destructive behavior on the part of
teenagers.

The noted pediatrician Dr. Benjamin Spock,
writing in the October 1979 issue of *Redbook*
magazine, further describes the far-reaching effects of divorce upon children. According to Dr.

Spock, children two to four years old show regressive behavior in toilet training, whine and cry, are irritable, throw tantrums, have sleep problems and are aggressive when parents are in conflict.

Five- and six-year-olds exhibit traits of anxiety and aggressiveness. Sorrow sets in for the seven- and eight-year-olds, many of whom express a longing to spend more time with their fathers.

In discussing some of the research done in parent-child relationships among divorced families, Dr. Spock points out that tension is high between mother and son, and the departure of the father is most traumatic on children of preschool age.

Spock feels that the father's continued closeness to his children is of primary importance to the youngsters and to their adjustment. He is strongly in favor of joint custody for all parents who think they can summon the cooperation required.

Another expert in the field, Mel Roman, a professor of psychiatry, maintains that children are deeply pained by their father's absence and interpret it as abandonment. In an article for the *Conciliation Courts Review*, Roman asserted that these children feel deserted and guilty and have few ways to express their anger and confusion.

Roman further states that sole-custody mothers exhibit anger and often develop neurotic attachments to their children. They force sons into the role of substitute fathers and see daughters as appendages of themselves. Roman sees many psychological risks connected with sole custody. He has also had the painful experience of losing custody of his own children and has written an excellent book on the subject, *The Disposable Parent.*

The case of Robin and Steve B. illustrates Roman's point very clearly. After Steve left the home, Robin unconsciously placed a heavy burden on their twelve-year-old son. She began turning to him for advice, saying, "You're the man of the house now." She has delegated household repairs and maintenance to the boy and has centered her social life around him. She buys theater tickets and he is her escort. The child is overwhelmed by the responsibility.

Male Needs after Divorce

There has been little research done on the psychological effects of divorce on men. We have interviewed hundreds of fathers alone and in group sessions. They tell us they have many physical and emotional symptoms. Some men say they feel tired, depressed, and are incapable of making decisions or handling problems. There are those who tell of irritability, sleeplessness, apprehension, dissatisfaction with their careers, and grave doubts about their futures. Others deny the existence of physical problems. However, years later they recognize that their headaches, blurred vision, drowsiness and stomach problems were all caused directly by their divorce and separation from their families.

Mel Roman asserts that fathers do not walk away from their families carefree and unscathed and without severe physical and emotional problems. He goes on to say that his studies have "uncovered complaints of sudden and dramatic weight loss ranging from eight to 50 pounds, eye and dental problems which were diagnosed as nerve related, high blood pressure, rheumatoid arthritis, and psychosomatic complaints ranging from throbbing backache and footache to a man who believed he was having a recurrence of a collapsed lung."

These problems might not be as crushing if the male were able to deal with them in a secure setting. However, most men must handle drastic changes in their lifestyles, finances and parenting relationships at a very vulnerable time in their lives.

In Alvin Toffler's "future-shock" terms, the male is dispossessed of his stability zones. The combination of changes in residence, perhaps career, and certainly marital status are sometimes overwhelming.

One friend of ours, a well-to-do professional, had left a long marriage, three children and a lovely home. He had always had a full-time housekeeper and had never had to care for his own domestic needs before. The last time we saw our friend, he was eating dinner at an all-night hot dog stand at 11:00 P.M. Dessert was two glazed doughnuts. He talked about the problems he had been having in adjusting to a small apartment, learning to change linens and do his own laundry.

We have seen his apartment. There are stacks of newspapers along one wall, which he uses as chairs. He doesn't empty the overflowing ashtrays. He eats out when he runs out of clean dishes. His need for rehabilitation and nurturing through these emotionally disabling times is as great as any woman's.

The Nurturing Father

The major reason why there are so many fatherless households is that society in general, and the courts in particular, are unwilling to recognize the male's ability and need to nurture his children.

Eric Berne, author of *Transactional Analysis in Psychotherapy*, tells us that we all need positive strokes, such as pats on the back and compliments. We need structured time, closeness, and moments of intimacy. Human beings thrive on rituals, activities and pastimes. We also respond to negative strokes. Denials, discounting and criticism reduce our feeling of self-worth. According to Berne, we are fulfilled by caring and loving, by closeness and sharing. We are diminished when these things are withdrawn.

We must recognize that males share the same basic fundamental needs as females. Thus, the male also must give and receive affection; he also requires touching, closeness and interaction with others. Fathers need to nurture, and children have an equal need to receive nurturing from their fathers as well as their mothers.

Many men think that women are born knowing how to be mothers. They feel inadequate to the task of caring for children. We were recently on a talk show when a male caller addressed a question to the female co-author of this book. His concern was how he could ask for custody, as he didn't know how to take care of a little girl. He said, "I don't know how to curl a little girl's hair." My reply was, "Neither do I, and I'm a woman." He was taken aback at this, but it happens to be the truth.

Even though I have two grown daughters, I never did learn how to do their hair. Furthermore, when I look back to my own childhood I realize that my mother never curled my hair either.

There are far more important things than hair curling, and most fathers are nurturers without their being aware of it. We see examples all about us every day. A walk through virtually any park, playground or toy store reveals much about fathers. It is usually the father who holds the back of the bike while his child teeters perilously on two wheels. It is often Dad who explains the mysteries of the strange and wonderful world at the zoo.

Frequently it is Dad who walks the floor at night with a colicky baby, who sits out the long hours in the doctor's waiting room, chauffeurs the kids to the orthodontist, and drives the car pool. Fathers are seen at school during open house, at recitals and graduations, and would probably be at PTA meetings if the meetings weren't held during business hours for the convenience of the ladies.

It is often Dad who sits beside his child on the first driving lesson, and who waits up after the school prom. How many fathers have memorized the lines from dozens of Dr. Seuss books while reading the kids to sleep? It's often Dad who bandages skinned elbows, kisses sore knees, combs tangles out of hair and gently wipes away tears from grimy faces.

Men are capable of running the washing machine, the dishwasher and the vacuum. They can prepare meals, change diapers, write notes to the teacher and do everything else that is required of a parent. When the kids are out at night, men feel the same panic at a late phone call as women do.

Dads certainly are able to feel the same pride and joy as Moms when they watch their child's ballet recital. They feel the same satisfaction when someone compliments them on their "darling baby." In short, men are as willing and able to be parents as women.

The obvious question, then, is, why doesn't

society put the same value on fathering as on mothering? Why do we place a premium on "motherhood and apple pie," but not on "fatherhood and cherry pie"?

There are a lot of answers to this question. Basically our composite social biases are made up of countless individual attitudes. The way each male views himself forms a collective picture by which all males are viewed. Men have been taught over the years to see themselves as providers and not as nurturers. They have learned to play down outward displays of emotion. They know that women's place is in the home and men's place is at the office. After all, that's the way it has always been. Men accept that fathers are the disciplinarians and mothers are the ones who "kiss it and make it well." This has been so deeply ingrained that no one recognizes the signs that say it simply isn't so.

There is no doubt in our minds that many men are not only capable of being nurturing, but actively seek it and will forego highly successful careers to play the role of primary parent in their children's lives. In the past, men took on the role of nurturing parent only by accident or after a death in the family. Today many men are fighting for custody and once it is gained play a full role in the lives of their children.

Take the case of a man we met shortly after the onset of his divorce. This man is a high-powered executive. He makes major decisions and deals with the rough-and-tumble world of high finance. He was known as tough, unbending and extremely competent. He spent most of his time building his career until the divorce.

Today the change in him is incredible. This tough executive, after a bitter court battle that cost many thousands of dollars, has gained custody of his two little girls, ages three and five. He has become a soft, gentle, caring person. His life revolves around the children to the exclusion of his work and his social life. He says he has never been happier.

He cancels business appointments, breaks dates and builds his calendar around the two girls. His daughters can be heard in the background, giggling, crying or singing, while he is conducting business from his home.

Another father, a very successful CPA, has also changed his life to accommodate to his children. Before the divorce, clients could call him at the office or at home and get his undivided attention. Now it is very different. When he is talking to a client, he has been known to drop the phone in the middle of a discussion of capital gains to referee a fight between his two kids. Their needs come first.

Some men bring their children to monthly meetings of fathers' groups, so the kids will understand what their fathers are going through in order to spend time with them. One father bragged about taking his child onto a major construction site so she could see firsthand how the plumbing and electrical systems were put together for a high-rise building. Another took his child to several important high-level Washington meetings so his son could see the way Washington decision making takes place.

We have a friend whom we have never seen without his kids in tow. He is rather well-to-do and the baby-sitting facilities at his disposal would be the envy of any mother. But he feels it is important to be close to his children whenever they are with him.

After divorce there are many arrangements which can keep fathers in their children's lives. Sole-custody arrangements by their very definition exclude either the mother or the father from the nurturing relationship, and thus are not in the child's best interests. Our personal observations and research by others clearly show that joint physical and legal custody is in the best interests of all concerned.

The Custody Crisis

6

Since there is usually a great deal of hostility, bitterness and distrust between divorcing spouses, working out satisfactory joint-custody arrangements is a difficult task. However, divorced couples who have made joint custody work tell us it has been a very positive force in their lives.

In order to make joint custody viable, it is vital that the children not be used as weapons of war. The parents must put aside their own deeply felt anger, hostility, resentment and other destructive feelings in the best interests of their children. Parents who have succeeded have nothing but praise for joint custody.

Many people do not recognize the merits of counseling. They may think that if counseling failed to keep their marriage together it is of little value. Post-divorce counseling, however, can be very useful in unraveling financial and domestic affairs. It can be vital where there are custody disputes. We have interviewed many couples who reluctantly went into counseling after being ordered to do so by the Court. They come out singing its praises.

Through counseling couples are able to work out a set of clearly defined rules and a structured agreement for handling the children. At the beginning a rather rigid set of rules may be established which later, as cooperation and trust develop, may be relaxed and made more flexible.

Most child-custody arrangements are in the form of court orders. These may range from loosely worded documents granting "reasonable visitation" or allowing both parents to share custody, to lengthy documents specifying times and places, and defining the legal, physical, financial, and even moral obligations of the parents. Many parents develop workable arrangements which may have little resemblance to the original court order, but since both recognize the merits of cooperation, there is no legal challenge and the entire family benefits.

Divorcing spouses should have a clear understanding of what is involved in the different forms of custody. Various definitions of custody are often written in "legalese" and are hard to understand. We are going to define some common custody arrangements which you may find helpful.

The list below moves from sole custody, which excludes one parent, to co-parenting, which involves an ongoing and interactive relationship between both parents and their children.

Custody. Custody is the immediate charge or control exercised by one person over another. With respect to child custody, it includes the duties, rights or privileges a parent exercises over offspring. Natural parents have an equal responsibility to guard and preserve the physical and emotional well-being of their children.

Sole custody. In sole custody all of the rights, duties and obligations for the physical, emotional and psychological well-being of an offspring are vested in one parent. In granting sole custody the court may award visitation to the other parent. This grants the excluded parent the right to see, visit or talk to the child, but denies him decision-making authority or physical control over the acts of the child.

Sole custody has many limitations. It places a heavy burden on one parent while reducing the status of the other parent to that of a visitor. Sole custody is frequently awarded by the courts because it is expedient and easy to administer.

Sole custody enables one parent to exercise full control and dominion without the necessity of arriving at a consensus with the excluded parent. It places disproportionate responsibilities and power in the hands of one parent. Sole custody creates hostility and emotional deprivation. Unfortunately, most courts still grant sole custody routinely.

Split custody. Split custody is sole custody

in another guise. In this arrangement, each parent is given sole custody of one or more of the children. Traditionally, girls go with Mother and boys go with Dad.

In split-custody arrangements, each parent exercises full control and authority over the child or children in his or her care. This arrangement is, again, expedient. Little court time is required to break up families and to parcel out the parts much as one does in the property settlement.

Split-custody arrangements suffer the same limitations as sole custody, perhaps more so. Unless there are exceptional circumstances, it is not a preferred arrangement. Many parents complain that the presence of one child does not make up for the loss of the other. The children suffer the most, because they lose not only a parent, but their siblings as well.

Divided (alternating) custody. In divided or alternating custody, the time spent with each parent is divided into finite blocks. The custodial parent exercises exclusive control whenever the children are with that parent. The other parent has visitor status.

This arrangement is preferable to sole or split custody in that the children have access to both parents. Again, since the Court does not need to lay down rules, patterns of behavior, or means of resolving conflicts, divided custody is granted because it is expedient.

This form of custody is undesirable since it lacks continuity. This frustrates planned, long-term growth and a consistency of lifestyle that may not be in the family's best interests. For example, if the child starts orthodonture while with one parent, who pays for it and what happens if problems develop?

Joint custody. Joint custody is sometimes known as "shared custody," "co-custody" or "concurrent custody." These terms suffer from a lack of clear definition of specifics. On the surface they suggest a mutual involvement of both parents. The child's time is divided between both parents, and it looks as if there is a sharing of responsibility. In reality, sharing may not exist.

Many "enlightened" judges will grant joint custody or co-custody. The decree makes no effort to define how the physical time of the child shall be shared, or who shall be responsible for the legal, educational, religious, and medical decisions related to the child. Unless clearly defined, joint custody may not be workable.

More than one father has spent thousands of dollars fighting for joint custody, only to find that he has won nothing. What happens is that the child's physical residence remains with the mother while the father still has no real voice in the child's upbringing.

Let us now describe some more clearly defined forms of joint custody. These are more workable, since they address specific issues.

Joint legal custody. In joint legal custody, legal responsibility is shared equally by both parents, while physical custody is given to one parent. This form of custody often winds up to be the worst arrangement of all for the parent who does not have physical custody. The physical-custody parent has authority to decide on the living arrangements, hours the child will keep, selection of friends and recreational and health habits. The parent who has joint legal custody may still be denied visitation, even though he is legally responsible for the child's financial well-being.

In many states the father is legally liable for any lawsuits his child may be involved in. The father's income, assets, and even the income of his new spouse may be jeopardized by the careless actions of his child.

Joint physical custody. In joint physical custody both parents share on a relatively equal basis the physical control of the child, while the legal control is vested in only one parent. The child may spend several weeks or perhaps months with one parent and then go to the other. However, one parent has full legal custody.

This arrangement, while it provides physical access to both parents, is fraught with problems. The custodial parent who does not have legal custody may find himself in a situation where he cannot make important decisions which may be needed at the moment. He must go to the legal guardian with respect to any significant educational, medical, dental, legal or religious decision.

When in his physical custody, the child is only a guest. It is demeaning for a natural parent to have to seek permission from the other parent to sign a report card or fill his child's prescription.

Joint physical and legal custody. Joint physical and legal custody is sometimes called "co-parenting." It is based upon consensus and equality. This arrangement assumes that the wishes and concerns of both parents will be considered in the child's upbringing.

A fundamental aspect of this arrangement is that there will be a relatively equal sharing of the child's time and financial needs. Both share equally in the legal decisions and responsibilities. In co-parenting there are no guardians, custodians or visitors. There are only parents.

Both parents must work together to arrive at mutually acceptable decisions concerning educational, medical, legal and religious matters. The child cannot be used in a power play by one parent, or as a lever to extract alimony or excessive child support.

If there is a disparity in earning power between the parents, the most able one is expected to provide the greater portion of the child's support. It may happen that a wealthy woman pays substantially more of the child's support than a less affluent man.

A fundamental premise of joint physical and legal custody is that there will be a roughly equal sharing of time and access to the child. A child may spend part of the week with one parent and part with the other. Or one semester may be spent with a parent, with the child moving to the other one at the end of the period. There are a variety of arrangements that can be worked out.

At no time is the child considered to be "visiting" a parent. Rather, there is an ongoing parenting relationship with both divorced spouses. The child is made to feel that there are two homes and two caring parents. Either parent can sign the driver's permit and the report card. And, yes, there are two teddy bears and two ragged blue blankets, one in each home.

The California Joint-Custody Law

In January of 1980, California enacted one of the most far-reaching and progressive child-custody laws in the nation. The old law granted sole custody almost exclusively. In practice, mothers got custody virtually all of the time. The new law states that it is in the best interests of minor children to have frequent and continuing contact with both parents. It encourages parents to share the rights and responsibilities of child rearing.

Some of the important provisions of the law are worth mentioning here. If the child is of sufficient age and capacity to reason, and can form an intelligent preference, the Court shall give due weight to the wishes of the child. The sex of the parent shall not weigh in the judge's decision.

In cases where circumstances call for sole custody, the Court shall consider which parent is more likely to allow the child frequent and continuing contact with the other parent, and this parent shall be granted custody. If the judge does grant sole custody, the reasons for this decision must be put in the record. This is of great help if an appeal is made.

The new law charges the Conciliation Court with implementing a joint-custody plan, and with resolving any controversies which may arise. Another important provision is that both parents shall have full access to the child's records and information, including but not limited to medical, dental and school records.

The new California law puts both parents on an equal footing. Members of fathers'-rights groups joined with other men's-rights groups and professionals to put this law on the books. While it is too soon to assess the full impact of this law, some facts are clear. Judges who have granted joint custody are finding that fewer of these parents are coming back to the courtroom to settle disputes. There is a greater reliance on the conciliation process.

Finally, New York and other states are beginning to move aggressively on similar legislation, since its merits are obvious.

Co-Parenting Arrangements

Co-parenting is by far the preferred custody arrangement. Many parents do not realize that there are a variety of workable alternatives to help them share responsibility. Let's go over five distinct arrangements that have been found workable by many parents. Co-parenting is by no means limited to these. Many parents have found other creative solutions to their custody problems.

Implicit in these arrangements is a willingness to cooperate, placement of the child's best interests over the parents' hostility, equal sharing of the legal responsibility, and roughly equal division of the child's physical presence.

Type 1 (small fixed block). In this arrangement, the child moves back and forth between the residences of both parents in roughly equal fixed-time blocks. For example, a child may spend three-and-a-half days with one parent and three-and-a-half days with the other. A variation is four days with one parent and three days with the other, reversing the schedule the following week. Some parents find that a split of weekdays and weekends or alternating one week with each parent also works well.

The child remains in close proximity to both parents and the transition may be made after school or at the end of the week. The children we have interviewed tell us they like and feel comfortable with this arrangement.

Here is how Susan and Bill L. have worked it out. On Wednesday afternoon Bill leaves the office early to pick up seven-year-old Randi from school. She remains with him through Saturday. Sunday morning he drops Randi off at her mother's place where she stays until the following Wednesday, when the cycle is repeated. Randi has her own room, clothing and toys at each residence and has made many friends in both neighborhoods.

While there is still much bitterness between Susan and Bill, particularly since he has remarried, they both realize that Randi is happier with this arrangement than she would be if she couldn't see one of them. They consult when necessary, but keep it to a minimum and only when it concerns Randi. This summer they expect to alternate on a weekly basis because it is convenient.

Type 2 (large fixed block). The child moves back and forth between the residences of the parents in roughly equal large blocks of time. The child may spend three or four months with one parent and then go to the other. Sometimes the child moves back and forth on a semester or even annual basis. During the time the child is with one parent, the alternate parent has some weekends and evenings.

Gary and Elaine D. have worked out an arrangement based upon school semesters. Eleven-year-old Greg's school is close enough to both homes so that the parents can transport him. When Greg's primary residence is with

Dad, he is car-pooled throughout the week. He spends weekends or occasional holidays with his mom. On the alternate semester his primary residence is with Mother, and he spends weekends and some holidays with Dad.

Both parents are pleased with the schedule because it allows them a great deal of freedom, yet they still get to see their son frequently. Greg's work in school has improved since the animosity between his parents has subsided.

Type 3 (variable block). In the variable-block arrangement, the child moves back and forth between the residences of both parents in varying blocks of time. These time blocks may be based upon the job commitments of the parents or special interests and activities of the child. While the blocks are not uniform in length, over a period of time they balance out. Neither parent expects these time blocks to balance out to the day.

Howard and Joyce M. have been divorced for six years and have a fourteen-year-old son, Scott, who is very interested in camping. Howard is a film editor who, when employed, works seven days a week for many months. When there is a hiatus, he may be off work for an unpredictable length of time. The arrangement they have worked out is that when Howard is working, Scott stays with Joyce, and when Howard is off, Scott moves to his place.

Scott goes on extended camping trips with Joyce's brother, which gives both parents a break. Experience has shown that the time split, while not exactly equal, and tending to favor Joyce, is the best for Scott and his interests, and is the most practical for all.

Type 4 (unstructured movement). In this plan there is an unstructured movement of the child between the households of both parents. No effort is made to formally structure the time division or restrict the movement of the child between the two households. The only constraint is that the amount of time spent with each parent be roughly equal. This plan requires flexibility and good communication.

Unstructured movement works best where parents live close to each other, such as on the same street or in the same housing complex. It also works well where there are older children who have access to an automobile or bicycle.

Glen and Donna V. were sure this arrangement wouldn't work. They began with a carefully structured fixed-time block in which their daughter Nikki alternated between the two households.

Before the divorce Glen and Donna had purchased two condominiums, one for their own residence and one for speculation. After the divorce, each took one of the condominiums, which were in the same complex. At first this was very frustrating for Glen, as he saw Donna in the common areas with her new boyfriend. When he remarried, his hostility lessened.

Their thirteen-year-old daughter would not go along with the rigid structure they had worked out, but went where she pleased. After a while it became apparent that this free movement was in everyone's best interests. There have been problems, like the day Glen and Donna each expected the other to pick Nikki up at the beach. When neither showed up, Nikki came home by bus, very upset. Now they have better communication and rely upon notes and bulletin boards in both apartments to keep their schedules straight.

Type 5 (parental movement). When there are very young children it is sometimes preferable to keep the kids stationary while the parents move. The child remains in a common household and the parents alternate moving from this household to either a commonly held apartment or their own separate homes.

This arrangement is particularly suited to parents who can afford a housekeeper or live-in maid and provides a continuity in the child's life. There is a lack of privacy, however, since the divorced spouses must share a residence.

Take the case of Bernice and David R. They had settled into a suburban ranch house with their twin baby girls when the divorce took place. Bernice moved out into a one-bedroom apartment in the same neighborhood. She found this suitable since she could be away from the children while studying for her teaching credential. The babies stayed at home with David, and Bernice visited them regularly. The housekeeper took care of the children while David was at work.

During semester breaks Bernice moves into the house and David moves to a small apartment of his own. This arrangement usually works when the children are very young. It helps get past the infant or toddler stage, in which moving about is difficult for the children.

Spelling Out Terms

It is very important that joint-custody agreements be worked out in detail and put in writing. Many parents have wound up back in court because attorneys have used terms such as "reasonable," "usual" or "customary." Effective joint-custody agreements are those which spell out in detail all the rights, responsibilities and duties of the parties.

There are a variety of sources that parents can turn to to help draft workable joint-custody agreements. Attorneys tend to write complicated documents that go back and forth between them and require endless revisions. A better source is your local Conciliation Court counselor. Another excellent resource is *Joint Custody, A Handbook for Judges, Lawyers and Counselors*, available from the Association of Family Conciliation Courts, 10015 S.W. Terwilliger Boulevard, Portland, Oregon 97219.

Listed below are some of the major elements which should be included or resolved in your written agreement.

Responsibilities of the parties. The agreement should cite the legal and parental responsibilities of the parties. It should specify who will handle emergencies and what kinds and types of decisions will be made by each party. It should specifically address disciplinary, educational, religious, medical, dental and similar decisions.

Time sharing. The agreement should be specific as to how the physical custody of the child is to be divided. It should describe with whom the child will spend holidays, vacations, weekends, and for what period of time. Some of the best agreements spell out arrangements for all holidays, school vacations, birthdays, family activities, and any exceptions that might arise.

Exchange of information. An extremely important element in custody agreements is the exchange of vital information related to the child. The agreement should provide for the routine and periodic exchange of such information as medical records, school report cards, and other important information. This may be achieved without face-to-face meetings. But there should be some method outlined for decision-making conferences.

Economic arrangements. The agreement should cite the financial responsibilities of both parties. It should describe how routine and nonroutine financial matters are to be handled.

Such considerations as amount and date due of child support, tax matters, inspection of records, medical insurance, bills, and clothing should be outlined. Inability to meet financial responsibilities and procedures for back payment should be described.

Legal responsibilities. Since the intent of co-parenting is to share the legal responsibilities, it is important that these be described explicitly in the agreement. Such matters as inheritance, payment of legal awards or judgments, signing on bank accounts, etc., should be resolved.

Religious and educational considerations. The agreement should define who shall make religious and educational decisions. Items related to selection of school, choice of church, and attendance at church should be included.

Conduct and discipline. Parents often differ in their views on conduct and discipline of children. It is as important to define these standards and the responsibility of parents in these matters after divorce as before.

Movement of the parties. The agreement should state the limits and constraints on the parent who is caring for the child at any given time. While co-parenting implies equality, there may be instances where one parent must travel to visit the child. The agreement should indicate who is to pay for transportation costs of either the visiting parent or the child.

Recreation and travel. Provision should be included for the child's recreational and travel needs, such as summer camp and trips abroad.

The arrangement should be clear as to funding for these situations.

Conflict resolution.   A vital aspect of custody agreements is the provision for resolving impasses. The agreement should specify how mediation or arbitration is to be used in conflict resolution. It should state who shall pay for these services, when they can be triggered into action, and who shall select the service.

It may sound like all of this is a lot of legalese, which will only breed confusion and litigation. However, many co-parents have told us that they have been able to avoid problems and frustrations because the terms and conditions of custody were clearly defined. A delicate balance must be maintained between flexibility and specificity. If there is any doubt, it is preferable to lean toward being specific. Rules can always be relaxed later.

Games
Kids Play

7

"I don't want you to marry Jim. I hate him! I hate him! I want you to marry Daddy!" sobbed six-year-old Cindy.

"But, honey, Jim has been good to you. Remember the bicycle he bought you last Christmas?"

"I don't care! I don't want him to be my daddy!"

Ellen's heart was heavy as she and Jim discussed the problem. "I don't know what to do! I love you, but she's my little girl and I don't want to hurt her."

This is a situation that many divorced parents with children face. Most people do not recognize or understand the deep psychological undertones and psychodynamics which are at work here. In this chapter we look at the games kids play and the relationships between parents, stepparents and children.

Many parents are willing to examine the financial problems divorce brings but are unable to deal with the emotional effects upon their children and themselves. They view children as only innocent victims of divorce and are unwilling to see them as negative forces and sometimes prime motivators. More than one marriage has hit the rocks because children have consciously or unconsciously stirred up wrath or friction between parents.

We may be castigated for our views, particularly in light of the reverence the courts, the law and society show toward children. But the hard fact is that the best interests of the children almost always overshadow the best interests of the family and may break the hearts of one or both parents.

There is much unconscious and sometimes conscious action on the part of children that can create many problems for couples. This comes into play at traumatic times such as divorce, separation, remarriage or the death of a family member. Children are often greatly traumatized during these difficult times. It is because they are suffering so much that no one recognizes their actions as being destructive.

Family Psychodynamics

Those who have worked closely with parents before and after divorce recognize the complex psychodynamics at work within the family. We often see games, gambits, strategies, and ploys used by both parents and children to gain their ends. The basic manipulation of power within the framework of the family takes different forms.

Prior to a divorce, there is usually equality between parents. That is, husband and wife have an equal say in child-rearing decisions such as education, medical treatment, discipline and the like. The courts recognize this equality of parenthood. Children, prior to a divorce, have little say in household matters. The child is generally subject to the rules laid down by the parents. The courts recognize a parent's right to make decisions and establish rules governing the physical and financial welfare of the child.

Simply stated, parents share the top of the hierarchy equally and the children are subordinate and hold virtually no power. It is assumed the parents care for and will look out for their children's best interests.

The moment a separation or divorce takes place, however, there is a radical shifting of the power elements within the family. As soon as papers are served, the father tends to be excluded from the household and loses his place at the top of the hierarchy. The mother is no longer an equal, but gains a strategic advantage because she has the sole decision-making power. This is enforced by our legal system.

There is a 180-degree shift in power with respect to the children. Children, who prior to the divorce or separation were pawns, now take on power. The child's preference becomes a key element in the power play. The courts respect the wishes of the child in making custody decisions, which often affect the financial structure of the settlement. Both parents often curry the favor of the children to gain the upper hand. Thus the divorce effectively restructures the power, placing family members in a new hierarchy, with the children on top.

Big Power in Little Hands

Psychologists have given us insight into the adverse effects on children when a divorce takes place. We know that children suffer from guilt and insecurity. They feel unloved and as if their needs are not being considered. We do not wish to deny these feelings or diminish their importance. But it is equally necessary to consider the feelings and needs of the adults as well. It is not equitable to place one family member above the rest. The family should be considered as individual human beings, with each member's emotional well-being having equal value.

Let's take a closer look at some of the conscious and unconscious games children play and the means by which they exert power and pressure upon parents. First let's examine some of the psychological aspects of divorce and how pride and self-respect, or guilt, insecurity, and selfishness come into play.

Children are astute at sensing a parent's feelings. They may use a parent's guilt and insecurity as weapons. Children often manipulate their parents by turning feelings of pride, self-respect and "parenting instinct" to their own advantage. These are very powerful forces, which few people are willing to recognize.

Here are some of the ways in which children exercise power. One way is to engage in intra-family politics. Ben R. and his brother Carl had exhibited intense sibling rivalry since they were kids. When Ben's divorce took place, his fourteen-year-old son, Josh, turned to Carl and made untrue statements about Ben that exacerbated the problems between the brothers. Carl was only too happy to hear these stories and did not need much encouragement to side with Josh. This also gave Carl an excuse to side with Ben's ex-wife, Laura. Josh felt important, since he was now the center of attention.

When Ben tried to enforce discipline upon Josh or when he denied him anything, Josh went to Carl with his grievances. Ben had to fight his son, brother and ex-wife on every point and always lost.

Some children use their power to derail a new relationship. Eight-year-old Tony came close to breaking up the marriage of his mother and her new husband. Tony made up lies about his mother and stepfather and went from one to the other with these stories. Even though the stories were obviously untrue, there was much tension in the household. This intensified a split which had already developed because the child was taking an inordinate amount of his mother's time and attention.

Children are often quick to exploit their parents financially. Thirteen-year-old Kelly was able to extract a new stereo and about $100 worth of records and tapes out of her father. She told him about all the things her mother was buying her and he felt he had to compete. Then he found out that Kelly got an expensive ski outfit from her mother by telling her about the stereo.

Kids are also quick to sense differences between their parents' perceptions of discipline. One mother complained about the problems she had disciplining her fifteen-year-old twins. She had custody of the two boys and they kept telling her she was too strict and they liked being with Dad better. In order not to play the heavy she relaxed her standards. Then they went to their father and told him, "Mom lets us do this when we are with her. How come we can't do it here?"

Getting Attention

Children are smarter than we think. They communicate their feelings and needs both verbally and nonverbally. They demand a great deal from their parents. Children have a great need to be parented. They need to have limits set on their behavior. Many of their destructive actions are in reality cries for help. During a divorce, children are extremely insecure. They are faced with the loss of stability and a change in their familiar surroundings.

Parents are so involved with their own misery that they often overlook the emotional deprivation their children are suffering. Frequently the children will act in a way which forces their parents to set limits or at the very least to acknowledge that the children count. If the children are left without parental involvement, the burden of controlling their own behavior is overwhelming. When their parents abandon them emotionally, the children fear that they will be abandoned physically as well. This is at the heart of much of the child's negative and destructive behavior during and following a divorce.

Let's look at some of the ways children act out their fears in their cries for help:

The silent treatment is one way. Jimmy stopped talking to his father for a year and a half. He refused to go with his dad on visitation days and wouldn't even talk to him on the phone. Jimmy was full of guilt and anger. He did not understand the fact that his dad's leaving was involuntary. Jimmy felt abandoned and alone because of the divorce. The silent treatment was Jimmy's way of protecting himself against further hurt, and was at the same time an expression of anger against his father.

Bad language and slovenly personal hygiene are two common means of crying out for help. Children refuse to take baths, brush their teeth or comb their hair, and may wear the same pair of grubby jeans for two weeks. They are bewildered by what has happened. They do not understand their own feelings, but they know they are hurting. They persist in this antisocial behavior because it gets a response from their parents.

Children may become sullen or introverted. They may become hypochondriacs or engage in over- or undereating as a means of getting attention. Others express anger, guilt or hostility by using drugs or alcohol, or by driving recklessly.

Finally, there are the children who behave as if nothing had happened. They go through the traumatic period of divorce seemingly unruffled. Inside there is an emotional hurricane. These children are often the most difficult to deal with. It is easy for parents to assume that the children are "taking it well." That way they can avoid dealing with the emotional problems their children are having.

Young Children

Young children deal with the insecurity and emotions caused by a divorce in their own way. It is frequently the young children who are the most deeply hurt because they do not understand what is happening. They know that their lives have changed. Often one parent is no longer around.

Some children feel ashamed that their father doesn't live at home anymore. One six-year-old youngster told his friends that his father was a senator and was always away in Washington. The subterfuge worked until his friends grew older and began asking questions. The child was further embarrassed when his deception became known.

Many young children maintain the fantasy that their parents will get back together. Sometimes they think that if they are very, very good, their daddy will come home to live again. Some children develop stomachaches, headaches, nausea or other complaints, fantasizing that their parents will have a happy reunion at their bedside.

Preteens

As children grow older, they engage in more sophisticated ploys and behavior. Preteen children are good at playing upon their parents' feelings of guilt or inadequacy. For instance, a father may be continually reminded by his twelve-year-old that he walked out on the family. A woman may be told that Dad wouldn't have left if she had only behaved differently.

It is not uncommon for recently divorced or separated spouses to have a great deal of curiosity and interest in the affairs of the ex-partner. They want to know who their former spouses are dating, where they go, what friends they see, and so on. Parents often try to pump their children for information. Some children use this curiosity to their advantage. The more sophisticated child will meter out desirable information. This gives the child the ability to manipulate and to maintain some control.

Taken to an excess, some children may tell outright lies, if the information they have does not give them enough control. Through this control, they can extract favorable treatment or gifts.

Teenagers and Young Adults

Teenagers are trying under the best of circumstances. Many of them are going through a difficult adolescence, and the trauma of divorce may be more than they can handle. The presence of a teenager in the home adds to the burden at the time of divorce. Many teenagers are masters of manipulation. They may sow the seeds of dissension in a new relationship by lying, forgetting to deliver messages on purpose, or delivering distorted messages, in order to create conflict. Frequently the children are jealous of a new spouse or lover and want their parent to themselves.

Teenagers are constantly testing their parents. During these years of growth, teenagers need to know that they have the same love and affection from their parents that their siblings have. This is sometimes translated into monetary terms. For instance, when Mark B. was sent to an out-of-state college, his brother Gary insisted that he also be sent away to school, even though he had always had his heart set on studying music at a local conservatory. This was his way of testing his parents. When they agreed that he also could go away to school, he backed down.

Young adults have their own ways of dealing with the trauma of divorce. Older children may understand the problems parents are going through but be of little help to them. Some will refuse to discuss the divorce or its effects on the parents or themselves. The subject is off limits. Even after the parents have healed their wounds, the older children may steadfastly stay out of any discussion of the divorce. Any attempt to involve them in a post-divorce relationship may only generate hostility.

It is interesting how a young adult's perception of events changes with time. A child's memory has a way of changing history. It may be hurtful for a father to hear his grown daughter say that he treated her selfishly when she was young, that he was only interested in his work and golf. In reality, he may have devoted a great deal of time to her, and he remembers a lot of happy hours spent doing things together. But to justify her hostility, which she really doesn't understand, it is necessary to twist the facts, albeit unconsciously.

Time has a way of healing even the most painful wounds. Given time, the pain lessens, the children mature, and better days lie ahead. Eventually the children learn to understand and deal with their own feelings, and their parents' as well. As children mature and form their own relationships, they may begin to develop a greater compassion and understanding for the problems their mother and father lived through.

During and immediately after a breakup there is a lot of hostility, exploitation and game playing. This usually subsides when families restructure and achieve an equilibrium. There are positive forces at work. Once a plateau or a period of stability has been reached, many families work actively to maintain the new status. Their fear of becoming embroiled in the problems of the past forces them to look more objectively at the present.

Kids and Their Games

Be aware of the feelings of the rest of the family during stressful times. Everyone concerned is experiencing a deeply felt pain. Be willing to communicate and remain open to the feelings and emotions of other family members. However, don't allow any one member of the family to be the scapegoat. It is easy to place blame on someone who is vulnerable. It is also easy to accept blame if you are feeling guilty.

If parents do not agree on how to handle a

problem child, a lot of accusations and guilt are generated. Take the case of Lois and Arthur M. Their marriage was on the rocks when they first started going to a marriage counselor. Lois accused Arthur of being too harsh with Billy, their fourteen-year-old son. Billy had been caught forging his parent's signature on his report card and also shoplifting from a local department store. He was threatening to drop out of school and had run away from home several times. Lois claimed it was all Arthur's fault because he made too many demands on Billy. She said he always lost his temper and didn't listen to Billy. Arthur denied this repeatedly. "I love Billy. I would never do anything to hurt him. Stop making me feel guilty!"

The therapist, who had been listening quietly, spoke up. "Arthur, why are you protesting? If her accusations are not true, then you have nothing to worry about. Nobody can make you guilty but yourself."

It wasn't until several hours later that the impact of what the therapist had said struck home. Arthur knew he was neither inconsiderate of nor overly harsh on Billy. He spent a great deal of time with his son. He felt confident that he had been a good father and had no cause to feel guilty. The moral is: don't accept guilt if you are innocent.

If you feel you have done something wrong, don't overcompensate. A few harsh words or an intemperate action may lead to an extensive effort to redress the wrong. Admit and correct your mistakes, but be reasonable. Nobody is perfect, even if our kids often expect us to be. If a situation is beyond your control, recognize and admit it, and get help. If the kids see they cannot manipulate you, they will respect you more and feel better about themselves.

Some of the most distressful family situations disappear given time. Teenagers grow up. Immature spouses may mature, with the help of some therapy. Hurt feelings heal. It is not necessary to win every game.

The Hired Guns

8

Brian left the courtroom shaking with rage and disbelief at what had just occurred. "I can't believe it," he muttered over and over. "I just can't believe it."

Brian had arrived at the courthouse that morning feeling fairly confident. He had apprised his attorney of all the facts concerning his wife's financial abilities, their expenses, and everything else he could think of. His wife had been working as a legal secretary during the preceding four years and her salary was only slightly less than his. She was asking for $500 a month alimony and $400 child support for each of their two children, but Brian was sure his attorney would convince the judge that this was unreasonable and uncalled-for. After all, he only brought home $1500 a month.

He arrived at the courthouse early, hoping to go over a few last-minute things he had thought of the night before. However, the attorney had not yet arrived. Brian paced nervously up and down the crowded hallway. Finally, ten minutes late, his lawyer appeared, apologetic and harried. Brian decided not to mention the things he had thought of because there wasn't time.

Finally Brian's case was called. The judge listened attentively for forty minutes to what the two attorneys had to say, asked a few questions, then made his decision. He ordered Brian to pay $350 a month alimony and $300 a month for each child. Brian sat stunned as his attorney gathered his papers together and said, "That's the breaks, kid."

"I don't understand it," said Brian. "He just gave her sixty-five percent of my salary. Why didn't you stress the fact that she makes almost as much as I do?"

"He knew," the lawyer replied, "because he had all the paperwork in front of him. He probably wanted to make sure she is protected in case she loses her job. I can't be responsible for what the judge does."

To the uninitiated, the attorney is a protector of your rights and is committed to work diligently in your best interests. Unfortunately, all too often it turns out that the man's attorney is his worst enemy. Indeed there are many honest lawyers practicing family law. But there are too many who are incompetent, careless, and insensitive to the male's problems.

We recently ran into an old friend whom we

hadn't seen for some time. He has been practicing family law for a number of years. He has never been divorced and has been married for twenty-three years. He mentioned that he had seen some of our writings and remarked, "You're banging your head against a stone wall. You can't change the system. How can people who couldn't agree while they were married ever agree on raising their children after divorce? Nobody can ever convince me that joint custody will work!"

Unfortunately, our friend is representative of the views of the majority of attorneys now practicing law. So we start this chapter off with a warning. One of the major criteria for choosing your attorney is, will he or she fight for your rights as a father with conviction? If your lawyer does not believe in your cause, the chances of winning your case are considerably diminished.

Lawyers are not miracle workers. They must work within the constraints of an archaic system, bound by rules and procedures which all too often inhibit the administration of justice. At best lawyers can only present a client's case and hope for a fair decision. Whether justice is forthcoming depends upon the biases or attitudes of the judge and the financial ability of the litigant to see his case through to the end.

It comes as a great surprise to many men that there is a disparity between the way the law is written and the way it is applied. Common sense and fairness do not necessarily play a part in the way the law is applied. A client is often advised by his attorney that going to court is a crapshoot, and presenting a good case doesn't guarantee a win.

Selecting an Attorney

One of the most critical phases in any divorce proceeding is the selection of an attorney. Many people choose a lawyer because he or she has handled business matters for them, or is a personal friend. The selection of a family-law attorney is probably as critical as the choice of a specialist for major surgery. In fact, dividing a family is a form of major surgery, and you should choose your attorney accordingly.

The average person who would not select a skin specialist to treat a broken arm, thinks nothing of going to a business-law expert with a divorce or custody problem. Family law is a complex, sophisticated, and changing legal art. It requires an attorney who knows the temperament and attitudes of the judges in the family-law courts. The lawyer should be able to deal with the psychological and emotional aspects which affect his client's decisions.

The adversary nature of the present family-law system requires that both sides be represented independently. This is because there is no longer a community of interests, but two discrete entities. Therefore it is not practical to try to save money by using the same lawyer. It is unfortunate that this is so, because the introduction of two opposing counsel in and of itself creates conflict.

Before engaging in a full-blown adversary conflict, couples should consider the total psychological and economic effects upon all of the parties. It is a good idea for divorcing spouses to develop some guidelines and a general settlement structure before involving attorneys too heavily. It is sometimes possible to lay out the basic division of property and child-custody arrangements before attorneys become involved. Many lawyers polarize parties if there is no basic agreement of positions. As the divorce moves forward, attorneys may be useful in detecting unfair or grossly disproportionate settlement offers. Both spouses should rely on fairness and sound judgment in making decisions. Some of the most complicated and disastrous legal battles have resulted where the spouses have turned over the decision- and policy-making aspects of their case to their lawyers.

There are attorneys who are more interested in building legal fees than in settling cases. These lawyers are called "fee builders." Fee builders begin by preparing a massive amount of unnecessary declarations and pleadings. They ask for what is known as "boxcar discovery." They may typically ask the opposing attorney to produce an enormous accumulation of

irrelevant papers and documents. They schedule lengthy and costly depositions. Points
which could be resolved by negotiation or a
simple request become major legal battles.
They subpoena documents that the other party
has volunteered to turn over willingly. Fee
builders prepare lengthy interrogatories (questions to be answered under oath) which run the
clock up unnecessarily.

Another type of attorney to avoid is the
"bomber." The bomber is bent on vanquishing
his opponent. He insists on a total win. He re-
fuses to compromise. Bombers advise their clients against signing settlements which require
giving in on some points even though it will
save the client time, money and aggravation in
the long run. They insist on winning every
point even if it means a long, drawn-out court
battle.

You can spot bombers or fee builders by their
attitudes in your early dealings with them. If
they seem more bent on winning than settling,
on fishing expeditions, boxcar discoveries or
just churning paper, you should think seriously
before retaining them. If one spouse selects a
bomber or fee builder, the other party is in trouble. He must engage in a defensive paperwork
war merely to protect himself. This proves to be
costly in both emotional and economic terms,
yet may be unavoidable.

Before you select an attorney, see him or her
in action. Don't take someone else's word for a

lawyer's ability or methods. Go to court and monitor his performance. Choose a family-law specialist and discuss his tactics. Above all, be sure he is on your side.

Some men's-rights groups have referral attorneys with whom they work closely. These lawyers are very sensitive to men's rights, divorce and custody problems. They should, however, be investigated carefully and not be taken at face value. Some attorneys affiliate themselves with men's-rights groups because of the large referral business and not because of their commitment to the cause of men's rights.

Rapport and Strategy

When you have chosen an attorney, you should work very closely with him or her and develop a satisfactory working rapport. Do not call after working hours unless it is a true emergency. Put things in writing rather than making a lengthy phone call. Be understanding of your lawyer's problems and particularly of his calendar commitments and case load. Remember, you are not his only client.

Most attorneys expect to lead their client's case, making decisions in the best interests of the client. They will drop a client who does not cooperate with them. On the other hand, there are clients who view their lawyers as merely mouthpieces. They expect to plan the strategy and ignore the wisdom and judgment of an experienced attorney.

A middle ground should be struck here. You should avoid unquestioningly following your attorney's advice. You should have all the facts and be part of the decision-making process. He may simply be taking an expedient route and be willing to give up points that are important to you. On the other hand, if you are overly directive with your attorney, he may put on a good show for you, but it won't hold up in court.

It is important for you and your attorney to agree on your goals. Some lawyers advise giving the adversary everything he or she asks for so that the matter can be settled with the least amount of legal expense and emotional conflict. This may appear very tempting if you haven't looked closely at what is being asked for. Some women ask for the kids, the house, the car, the furniture, the investments, high alimony, and everything else you own now and will own in the future. Men who accept this "easy way out" may spend the rest of their lives regretting their decision.

Tips and Pointers

Anyone who has been through extensive litigation has probably learned a lot about the system. The trouble is it often comes too late.

Some of the suggestions below may be difficult to carry out under the burden of emotional tension. But they are important and have been gathered together from the hard experiences of many men.

Keep a written chronology of events. Record such things as the date of separation, the date your attorney was retained, and all hearing dates, including the names of the judges, commissioners and, if possible, the name of the court reporter. You may need this information later. If you can afford it, you may want to obtain a written transcript of your hearings.

Keep a log of attorney visits and phone calls. Record the date, time and length of each visit, court appearance, or phone call. Also keep a record of your payments. Obtain a copy of the agreement or fee schedule you have agreed on with your lawyer. Some attorneys bill for flat blocks of time. Try to get a detailed accounting of how your lawyer's time was spent and reconcile this with your log. You will be surprised how many mistakes are made.

Many lawyers ask for a retainer when they first take on a new client. Ask your attorney to inform you when your retainer is used up. You may be surprised to find how quickly $1000 is used up with the clock running at $85 per hour or more.

Keep copies of all key documents, pleadings and records. Organize them chronologically in a binder. One binder may include copies of all legal documents. A second may include supporting letters, correspondence, memos, notes or other related data.

Be knowledgeable about your case. Don't assume that because you have hired an attorney, you can relax and all the details will be taken care of. Some clients prefer to study related case law and stay on top of their lawyer's legal strategy. If done judiciously, this can be helpful to your attorney and sometimes can draw things to his attention of which he was not aware.

Be honest with your attorney. If the opposing counsel springs some undisclosed information on your lawyer while he is in the courtroom, it can seriously damage your case. Some litigants hide assets from their attorneys because they fear higher legal fees will result. It's not wise to keep your attorney in the dark.

You may be very vulnerable if you have highly visible liquid assets. There are legal means of compromising your immediate cash position. You may pay off an automobile or house, or put your cash into a nonliquid form. You may prepay insurance, notes or mortgages. This will reduce the amount of cash available for distribution.

In other instances it may be advisable to convert as many community assets as possible into cash so that a division can be done easily and equitably. Discuss these alternatives with your attorney and decide which course is best for your circumstances.

A valuable tool which should be mentioned

here is the T-account. A T-account lists all assets based upon their present market value. There are two columns, one headed "husband" and the other "wife." This document is useful in distributing assets equally. You may wish to prepare several T-account statements describing various options. The object is to assign assets so that each party receives roughly half of the community estate.

Evaluating Your Attorney

It is important that you monitor and evaluate the performance of your attorney to be sure that he or she is working in your best interests. A good attorney pays close attention to detail and treats each client as an individual. He returns phone calls promptly and answers all letters and queries.

Your lawyer should keep you posted on the progress of your case. You should be sent copies of pleadings, settlement proposals and other pertinent documents and should always be closely involved in the decision-making process. Your bills should accurately reflect the time and expense put into your case.

A good attorney will be particularly sensitive to timing. He will know when to move aggressively and when to delay action. Many bad decisions are made by clients at a point when their lives are thrown out of balance. As an example, when the custody of children is at stake, some men may want to make concessions that are not in their best interests. A good lawyer will advise you against making decisions when he sees you are under emotional pressure.

Unfortunately not all attorneys are prepared by temperament or training to deal with the complex emotional and financial aspects of divorce. Justice Warren Burger has publicly stated that one-third to one-half of the nation's trial lawyers are incompetent. A lot of people feel this is an understatement. Recently, a Northeastern University law professor disclosed that forty-four percent of law-school graduates feel they are ill-trained to draft legal documents. Seventy-seven percent said they had not been trained to negotiate settlements, sixty-nine percent stated they had not learned how to counsel clients, and sixty percent felt their training had not prepared them to investigate facts.

Many people discover the incompetence of their lawyer after the statute of limitations on malpractice has run out. Generally, malpractice suits must be filed within one year from the time you discover that your attorney's actions or negligence have hurt you. To complicate matters, it is often difficult to find a lawyer who will represent you in a suit against another attorney.

Some lawyers talk tough when they are in their offices with only the client present. When they face the opposing counsel, however, they may be easily intimidated. Some attorneys fear the wrath of the judge and will go to great lengths not to offend him. They will more willingly compromise their client's best interests than offend the judge.

An example of gross misbehavior on the part of an attorney is exhibited in the story of Jason and Diane F. They had reached an impasse in their negotiations and decided to bring the case to court. Moments before the hearing, the judge ordered both attorneys into chambers without the clients present. The three of them worked out a settlement agreement which Jason felt was unacceptable to him, although his wife was quite pleased with it.

Jason told his lawyer he would not go along with the proposed agreement and wanted to litigate. His attorney replied, "It's too late. I've already agreed to the terms of this settlement offer. If you won't accept it, I'm going to walk off the case right now." Being inexperienced in legal matters, Jason felt forced to accept the terms offered, not realizing that the lawyer had used unreasonable pressure on him and in reality was ethically bound to represent his client's wishes.

Dismissing Your Attorney

Once you hire an attorney, you are not bound to keep him or her throughout the case, and in fact you are probably best advised to dismiss a lawyer you consider to be ineffective or incompetent.

If you have doubts about your lawyer's ability, there are several things you can do. First, discuss your concerns directly with him or her. If you do not get any satisfaction, it may be helpful to approach a senior member of the firm.

The ethics of the legal profession preclude your lawyer from holding your file hostage if there is any dispute. Your file must be released to you or your new attorney on demand. You are, of course, obligated to pay reasonable fees for services rendered.

If there is a dispute about the amount of fees due, or if you have a complaint about the quality of services you have received, report the matter to your local and state Bar Associations. These agencies are committed to look into the matter. You may not always obtain satisfaction, since the Bar Association is made up of attorneys rather than lay people. However, no lawyer wishes to have complaints filed with the Bar.

If there is cause, you may sue your lawyer either for malpractice or over disputed legal fees. While it is difficult to find attorneys willing to take on these suits, they can be found with some effort.

Finally, if you do reach an impasse in a dispute with your attorney, you may wish to consider arbitration. Many lawyers prefer resolving conflicts through arbitration rather than face their ex-client in court or before the Bar.

Changes in the system have been bitterly fought by Bar Associations. For example, a recent bill in California would have allowed for a summary divorce when the parties could work out a mutually satisfactory agreement. Parties would have been able to waive all rights to alimony, dispose of their personal property, debts, and real property in any amount without the aid of lawyers. This was vigorously fought by attorneys, who saw a lot of business going out the door. The final form of the bill allows for summary dissolutions only in marriages of less than two years. There must be negligible community property, and parties may not waive alimony.

Reform in the legal profession is slow to come. The present system is a money-making industry for attorneys, court reporters, investigators, court psychologists, and other related professionals. When reform does come, it will most likely come from the outside rather than from within the system itself.

The Prima Donnas of Family Law

9

The average law-abiding citizen rarely has occasion to see what goes on in a courtroom. Our impressions of what happens are gained from movies and television. We watch romanticized stereotypes which portray highly principled attorneys and kindly, white-haired judges. On television everyone is interested in seeing justice done.

Usually our first dealings with the real world of the courthouse take place when a divorce occurs. It is a tremendous shock to have our illusions shattered as if they had been hit by an atomic bomb.

Family-law courts are the stepchildren of the legal system. They are overburdened with litigants and inefficiently run. The system treats litigants with little regard for their suffering. The absence of outward manifestations of agony, such as screaming and blood, masks the pain. There is little privacy, and delicate personal matters are handled openly for any stranger to hear.

Here is the way Frank T. describes his first encounter with the court system. "I didn't expect to see the hallways jammed with so many people. Women holding babies and men in suits and ties, carrying thick files, filled the benches along the wall. Some people stood around in small groups, whispering to one another. When my lawyer arrived, he went over to my wife's attorney and shook his hand. He said something and they both laughed. I wondered what they said. I felt lousy."

Frank continued. "At 8:30 the doors of the courtroom opened and the horde of people moved in and took seats at random. It reminded me of a cattle call. The judge came in, took his seat, and then called the court to order. The bailiff started calling the cases. Alphonse vs. Alphonse,' he yelled. Two attorneys stood up and said, 'Ready for Petitioner,' 'Ready for Respondent.'

"I saw my wife, smiling and talking to the friend she had brought along for moral support. As we waited, the judge continued to call cases. I wondered what was going on. Later I found out that this was a Calendar Court judge, who only assigned the cases to available courtrooms. They didn't call my case until nearly noon. Then my lawyer and my wife's lawyer walked up to the bench. I heard the judge say, 'Go to Department 33, Judge Hill, 3:00 P.M.'

"In the hall, my attorney said that we would have to come back at 3:00 and we might as well have lunch. I wasn't hungry. We returned at 3:00 and went to Judge Hill's courtroom. I thought we would walk into an empty courtroom, with the judge ready to hear my case. Instead, a hearing was in progress and the room was full of strangers. At 3:30, the judge interrupted the proceedings and asked our attorneys to approach the bench. He said he wouldn't have time to hear our case today and wanted us to come back at 11:00 the next morning."

Later Frank was to find that it would be a day and a half before his case would actually be heard. He had to pay $1500 in legal fees while the attorneys sat around for two days waiting for their turn in a courtroom. Frank's experience is not unique. It happens every day in big-city courtrooms across the nation.

In smaller towns we see a different sort of family-law operation. Alan B.'s case illustrates another kind of problem. Alan's twelve-year marriage was scheduled for dissolution before the local Justice Court. Judge Crocker called the court to order. Tom Crocker was a golfing buddy of Alan's father-in-law. But Alan wasn't too worried because his attorney was a major contributor to the judge's reelection campaign. It appeared to Alan that the judge was listening attentively to all the testimony and his questions appeared to be objective. But when Judge Crocker announced his decision, it hit Alan between the eyes. The judge awarded sole custody of their two boys to Alan's wife. Alan would have to pay over sixty percent of his income in child support and alimony.

The judge also gave Alan's wife possession of the family home and the furniture. Alan got a note for $22,000, which would be payable in five years at eight percent interest. One year later Alan finds himself virtually penniless, living in a small, sparsely furnished apartment. He sees his children on alternate weekends and still owes $1800 to the two lawyers.

The Ruling Class

Judges have evolved into a ruling class as a consequence of our family-law system. They sit on the bench, wield massive power, and have wide discretion. Their word is law, and their decisions are not evaluated, monitored or reported to the electorate. The average person is helpless to challenge or question their rulings. Theoretically, there are mechanisms for appeal, but as a practical matter few can afford the time and expense to challenge an arbitrary decision.

The present family-law system does a serious disservice to both men and women and is exacerbating rather than solving marital conflicts. We have discussed the performance of judges with many attorneys and hundreds of litigants. Both winners and losers agree that there is a great deal of indifference, incompetence and lack of preparation and training among judges.

Family law lacks the glamour of other legal specialties and is mentally draining. The cases are fraught with emotion and hostility. Many judges lack the sensitivity and insight to deal with the emotional crises that the parties to a divorce face.

Most judges who sit in family-law courts have had legal training, but they lack an understanding of the role of counseling and therapy. Many of them have not taken courses in psychology, human relations, child growth and development, or other related disciplines. Very few judges have an understanding of accounting, real-estate principles, or other finance-oriented areas to help them deal with the complex money matters before them.

Some male judges have a deep dislike of women. This bias may be rooted in their early childhood relationships with their mothers, or may stem from an unrequited love affair. Whatever the source of their antipathy, it results in decisions that are generally pro-male. In other instances, a judge may feel overly protective towards all females. He will bend over backwards to see that women are taken care of. A judge's bias may come from his own feelings of insecurity or inadequacy. He may rail against a self-confident male litigant, or one whose demeanor or dress he sees as threatening. Again, the result is a biased decision. It is extremely rare for a judge to succeed in putting aside his prejudices in the courtroom.

Insensitivity is another characteristic to be dealt with. We gain an understanding of other people's problems when we experience them ourselves. Some judges have never been married, others have never been divorced. Some judges have no children, others are philanderers who do not have the need for close family ties. Without these personal experiences, they cannot empathize with those who come before them.

Judge S. is a case in point. He helped write divorce legislation and sat on the bench for many years. To those who know him personally it is obvious that he has a great dislike of women. He is in his early fifties, has never been married, and treats the women in his life shabbily. His friends' children irritate him and he doesn't mind saying so. This judge can never understand the trauma involved in divorce or child-custody matters. Yet he sits in our family-law courts, making decisions that affect the children, the lives, and the futures of thousands of men and women.

Abuses of Discretion

Many state legislatures go on the assumption that marriage, divorce and related matters should be treated differently than other civil or criminal legal affairs. Most states give judges wide discretionary power and latitude in family-law cases. Family law has become one big crapshoot. Some judges always order the family home sold. Others always assign it to the woman. Some judges grant lifelong alimony, others throw women on their own resources with a pittance. If you get a judge who favors your position, the luck of the draw is on your side.

Most civil matters follow rather carefully prescribed procedures and rules. An attempt at justice is provided through open court proceedings. Perjury is treated harshly and hearsay evidence is not allowed. Family-law courts, however, are a different matter. On the surface they appear to follow the same rules of evidence and constitutional procedural safeguards. But the latitude given the judge, combined with his personal feelings, often makes for unfair decisions. Of course you cannot litigate a broken heart with the same legal tools as a broken leg, and family law does require a specialized and unique set of rules. But there must be some structure and a reasonable amount of predictability.

One of the most abused aspects of family law is the conference held in chambers. The purpose of this informal meeting is to provide a nonadversarial, less hostile environment for negotiation and settlement. In practice, however, the client has no way of knowing what was said or whether his attorney adequately represented him. There is no court reporter present and no record of what took place. Thus his day in court is circumvented. Decisions made in chambers cannot be appealed, since appeals are based only on the written record, and there is none. Both men and women often feel that the results of these meetings are unsatisfactory.

Courtroom Strategy

There are some things you can do that will help you avoid many of the problems and pitfalls faced by litigants. Here are some of the key things to keep in mind as your case moves through the courts.

Have a clear-cut plan in mind and work out a strategy with your attorney. If you can reach an out-of-court settlement, you will be far ahead of the game. Before launching into extensive litigation, consider arbitration or mediation. If you cannot resolve your problems through conciliation, determine what you can realistically gain from going to court.

There is often much advantage gained from being the moving party, or the one who files first. The one who initiates the legal action may select the court as well as the time in which to litigate. Some men find they are served papers to appear at a place or a time not convenient to them. This can affect your job, and it is better for you to do the choosing.

You should be as knowledgeable as possible about court procedure and the attitude of the judge who will hear your case. Many men feel that it is helpful to sit in the judge's courtroom and watch him in action. Family-law courts are open to the public, and you may wish to attend several hearings prior to your own, so court procedure will be more familiar and less intimidating.

Sometimes your case will be heard by a commissioner rather than a judge. A commissioner is an individual appointed by a judge to fill available judicial positions. Judges are appointed by the governor of the state, or are elected. They are answerable to the public, while commissioners are answerable to the judges who hired them. Many people wonder whether it is better to have their cases heard by a judge or by a commissioner. There are those who express a strong preference for a judge. This is not necessarily a wise decision. If you have a choice, make your decision based upon the track record or performance of the individual, rather than on his formal status.

You should recognize the import of interim orders. These are called "Orders to Show Cause" (OSC's). An OSC is a preliminary-hearing order. At these hearings immediate matters such as protection of assets, temporary child support, custody or alimony are dealt with, pending the trial. Temporary orders have a way of becoming permanent solutions. Don't agree to temporary concessions which you cannot accept later as permanent.

Litigants should know the difference between a stipulation and a court order. A court order is a determination made by a judge, which is binding on both parties. It may be appealed on the basis of errors of law or fact. A stipulation is an agreement between two parties which has the effect of a contract once it is approved by the judge. You cannot appeal a stipulation, just as you cannot appeal a binding contract. Do not stipulate to any terms which are not acceptable to you.

It is important to build a good record at the trial stage in case you want to appeal. Be sure your attorney places on the record any objections or arguments which will support your position on appeal. Appeals are based on written records of the trial.

Litigation is costly and cheap is dear in the end. Don't try to save money by cutting legal corners which undermine your case. A low-priced, inexperienced or incompetent lawyer is no bargain. In fact, it could be the most expensive decision you ever made. If litigation is unavoidable, then get the best attorney you can afford and allow him the freedom to act in your best interests. Since judges frequently order the man to pay all or part of his wife's legal fees, many women go for the best. Your failure to hire an attorney of equal ability can prove costly.

Keep notes and records of each hearing. Write down the name of the judge who heard your case, the date it was heard, and the name of the court reporter. Obtain a copy of all minute orders or other legal documents produced by the hearing and review them. Keep a complete set of the pleadings. These are the legal papers upon which you base your arguments.

You should appear reasonable and in control of your emotions when in court. Dress appropriately, and don't shout, personally attack, or verbally abuse the attorneys, your wife, or the judge. Answer questions honestly but do not offer more information than is necessary. You do not have to hide the fact that you may be in a great deal of pain. Men have a tendency to hide their emotions and this sometimes appears to be a lack of caring.

Courtrooms are extremely intimidating. You may find yourself making concessions which you would not accept if you were in control. It is an emotional period, and you may find that the presence of friends or family will help boost your confidence.

It is not uncommon for hearings to be postponed or continued over many days. These are very trying times. You need your rest and as much moral support as you can muster. It is important for men to admit their feelings and to turn to other people for support and help.

Pro Per—Do It Yourself

The law allows for *pro per*, or do-it-yourself litigation. You may put on your own case in a family-law court. Some men who have had bitter experiences with lawyers strongly support *pro per,* but others disagree. Following are some of the pros and cons of handling your own divorce.

As your own attorney you will not have to pay your legal fees, though you will probably incur court costs. Win or lose, you may still wind up paying a contributory share of your adversary's legal bills.

You, better than anyone else, are familiar with the pertinent facts and details of your case. You will have to spend a great deal of time researching the legal points and authorities, if you hope to prevail. Since you are your only client, you can devote your full time and energy to your case.

Some judges go out of their way to help a *pro per* litigant. They lead him by the hand, since they know he is inexperienced in legal matters. This can prove very disconcerting to the opposing counsel, who will not receive the same treatment. But don't count on getting this kind of judge. The luck of the draw applies here also.

There are disadvantages in representing yourself. You probably do not know the law or your way through the legal jungle. You may find that your inexperience will be a source of great annoyance to the judge. You may overlook some vital points that an attorney could have used effectively. You may make procedural errors that will open the way to an appeal for your opponent. Finally, you lose the advantage of dealing through an intermediary. A lawyer can be an effective face-saving device to bring about compromise.

It is easy to lose your perspective when you are embroiled in litigation. In the adversary family-law system there are no winners, only losers. If you win your case, the victory may carry with it an exorbitant emotional and financial price. Your family may be alienated and your motives misunderstood. Giving up some of the points that you consider important may keep you from winning a Pyrrhic victory.

At some point in time you must put your hostility behind you. Some couples battle it out in the courts for years before realizing that they are ruining their lives. Only then do they let go of the past and begin to invest in the future.

Divorcing Our Court System

Family law is big business. There are vested interests which have a stake in the present system. Change will not come from within. History has proven that major reform movements always begin outside the system needing reform. The public needs to be sensitized to the problems in our family-law courts.

Many cases should not wind up in the courts at all. A method must be instituted to screen litigants who do not belong in the courts. They must be routed to arbitration, mediation or conciliation panels. When they do end up in court, attorneys should do their best to encourage settlements rather than adversary battles.

The quality of judges should be greatly improved. Only competent, trained and experienced judges should be permitted to handle family-law cases. The system of allowing judges to buy their appointments through contributions to political campaigns is intolerable, as is appointing unqualified people simply to fill quotas. We need a merit system based upon training and performance.

More emphasis must be placed on in-service training. Judges should be given ongoing instruction in psychology, human relations, accounting, and other related subjects. Their performances should be monitored.

Clear-cut guidelines should be laid down which define the limits of the court's discretion. It may be necessary, for example, to define the conditions under which a family dwelling must be sold. This would avoid the present custom of allowing the loose practice of selling homes in some cases and not in others. Judges should rely more on advice from mental-health professionals when dealing with emotionally distraught litigants.

There must be greater reliance upon modern electronic communications, word processing and computers in the courthouse. Improvements made in scheduling can save untold thousands of dollars in time and money. The computer can be used to schedule cases and allocate courtrooms. On-line terminals can provide reports, data and financial information. Attorneys can use beeper alerts so they don't have to sit in the halls wasting time. Forms and procedures should be streamlined, written in ordinary English, and should reflect equal treatment of both men and women.

It is interesting to speculate on what would happen if there were more women sitting on the bench in family-law courts. Perhaps more women would mean a turnaround from the present system which is biased against fathers and men. Yet there is no reason to believe that there would be an improvement if these women come from the same generation and are steeped in the same stereotypes as those now on our benches.

Hopefully there will soon be a new generation sitting as judges. These will be liberated men and women who think of people as equals and who may provide a solution to the problems now rampant in our courtrooms.

The Money Machine

10

Recently a young female executive took an important male client to dinner at an exclusive Los Angeles restaurant. They discussed the details of a pending business deal over martinis and then asked for the menu. The young woman looked at the menu and thought it peculiar that there were no prices listed. She commented on this to her companion, whereupon he remarked, "That's funny; mine has prices."

She beckoned the waiter, telling him there must be some mistake, as there were no prices on her menu. The waiter explained that it was the policy of the restaurant to give menus with prices only to their male customers. The waiter pointed out that it is French tradition that the man is expected to pay the bill and the woman shouldn't have to be concerned with money matters. He offered to break the rules and bring her a menu with prices, if she insisted.

The young executive rose, fuming, and said to her male companion, "Let's go somewhere else for dinner."

The next morning she angrily related the details to her attorney. She felt she had been humiliated in front of an important client. She decided to sue the restaurant, demanding they change their practice.

This case illustrates the deep-rooted financial stereotypes and expectations which society casts on both men and women. The man is the money machine and the woman is financially dependent. This assumption is the foundation on which the concept of alimony and child support is based.

The Economics of Being Male

For centuries the male has been a victim of this economic stereotyping. Men are unwilling to admit the existence of the unrealistic and demanding financial expectations which have been placed upon them by women and their families.

The wallet is the source of much anxiety and unhappiness for many men. This financial pressure is added to the heavy emotional and psychological burdens they face. A statement on men's rights is not complete without a discussion of financial expectations, financial role models, and the economic side of relationships.

Traditionally, a man's earnings belong to the family. Generally, all expenses are paid out of his salary, while the woman's earnings are considered supplementary. It is this "extra income" that buys the luxuries and the vacations. The tendency is to see the woman's income as frivolous and unimportant.

People feel uncomfortable if this basic stereotype is challenged. We are comfortable with the male as the giver and provider and the female as the taker and dependent. This attitude permeates our everyday social interaction. The man picks up the tab when they share a taxi. He pays the lunch check if they meet in a restaurant. He buys the theater tickets. And when the relationship is over, he is still expected to be responsible for her financial well-being.

There is a lag between social expectations and economic realities. According to a recent survey, twice as many women were working full time in 1980 as in 1970. By the year 2000 most women who are able to work will be employed. While women are not paid as well as men, they have nonetheless become a major force in our economy.

Money and Macho

People equate material things and economic success with masculinity and potency. Expensive cars, custom-made suits and shirts, designer labels, and other trappings of success are often used to hide a deep-seated insecurity. Many males feel they must exhibit their success for the world to see. Yet inside they are frightened children wondering how long they can keep up the pace required to make big money. Sometimes they can't. They drop dead, they have nervous breakdowns, they commit suicide, or they destroy their lives in some other way.

Another driving force which influences men's financial decisions is guilt. Even though it is usually a set of mutual problems which leads to the divorce, some men assume all of the blame. When the breakup occurs, they feel it is their responsibility to carry the financial load.

Even if he is the rejected partner, the man's conditioning does not allow him to walk away with financial equality. And our judges and attorneys reinforce this image of the male as the paying agent. They see men as simply an extension of their checkbooks, just as in the past women were seen as an extension of their cookbooks.

Living Together and "Palimony"

The highly publicized Marvin vs. Marvin case has established some important precedents and brought a new word into our vocabulary — "palimony." The decision not to marry no

longer protects a couple from the responsibilities of marriage. A binding contract can be
created by the simple act of living together. In
effect a couple can no longer choose not to
marry.

Lee and Michelle Marvin lived together for
six years, during which time he supported her
in a manner befitting a movie star's lady. She
even took his name. However, they explicitly
chose not to marry. When the falling-out came,
Michelle asked for $1.8 million in alimony and
substantial legal fees. Marvin balked. The case
went to the California Supreme Court and was
allowed to go to trial. Michelle ended up with
an award of $104,000, which is presently being
appealed.

Thus the courts have firmly established the
concept of palimony and "rehabilitation"
awards. This works against both males and
females. Christina Onassis paid dearly to be
free of her marriage to a young Russian man.
Rock star Rod Stewart paid actress Britt
Eklund a seven-figure settlement after a relationship of only two-and-a-half years. Nick
Nolte was sued for $5 million by his live-in love
of about seven or eight years. The willingness
of the courts to recognize live-in relationships
and implied contracts attests to the need for
clarifying the status of relationships with a
written document.

No other contract that people enter into has
more hidden strings than marriage. The average person goes into a marriage with little un-

derstanding of the legal and financial implications. They ask more meaningful questions when they sign a contract to buy a car than when they sign a marriage license.

Put It in Writing

It may seem unromantic to put things in writing, but today it is necessary. An enormous amount of litigation and frustration can be avoided if couples will clarify their expectations and agreements and put them down on paper.

There are few rules to guide you in establishing workable living arrangements. Some live-in couples establish a common purse, with each partner contributing an equal amount. Furniture and other expenses are paid out of this kitty. Others divide the financial responsibilities, with one partner paying certain expenses and the other paying the rest from separate earnings.

The purchase of a home or automobile complicates matters. Whatever course of action is followed, it should be fair and equitable and clearly understood by both parties. The arrangement should include provisions for disposition of assets and for resolution of disagreements.

If the couple decides to marry, it is advisable to draft a prenuptial agreement. There is far less pressure on the relationship when expectations are defined in advance. Marriage is a partnership. Anything that reduces conflicts and defines responsibilities and duties makes for a better and more secure relationship.

Severance Pay

A man in Chicago survived an attempt by his wife to have him murdered — and now she is insisting that he pay her alimony. She is asking for $500 a month and title to their $250,000 home.

Freddie Fields, a film producer, is paying $6000 a month alimony to a lady he was married to for only five months. They lived together for four years before they married. These are examples of modern-day marital "severance pay."

Alimony, its collection, duration and amount, is one of the major predicaments faced by males in our society today. Judges argue that there is a limited market for ex-wives in their middle or late forties with no record of paid employment. They say women put out to pasture need severance pay, now euphemistically called "spousal support." Attorneys are advised to tell their male clients to be prepared for a "long and continuing burden."

The roots of alimony go back to the days when women were treated as chattel. The male was responsible for his wife's welfare and was the conservator of all her assets.

Most courts today grant alimony based upon several factors, including the length of the marriage, the ability of one spouse to pay, and the need of the other. In marriages of long duration, this has generally meant that the male winds up paying substantial sums to his ex-wife for the rest of her life. He may be burdened with the loss of up to fifty percent of his post-divorce salary, and the female may be forced into a life of dishonesty and dependency.

In today's society men are no longer masters of the family estate. A substantial number of American women share equally in the financial decision making and economic fate of their lives. This sharing of the decision-making process forces a need for a close examination of alimony.

Some judges grant a "step-down" alimony schedule roughly equal to one-half the length of the marriage. Thereafter the wife is expected to become self-supporting. The present alimony system fosters much abuse. A spiteful ex-wife may ask for exorbitant alimony in order to punish her ex-husband. A husband may feel deep anger at the prospect of paying alimony to a wife who rejected him.

Lying and deceit are common where alimony is being received. Women hide their incomes, or the fact they are being supported by a boyfriend, to avoid loss of alimony. As a condition of receiving alimony, many men feel that the recipient should make available her federal income tax return.

Some judges order $1 a year alimony to self-supporting women just on the off chance that one day they may need to be taken care of by their ex-husbands. Many men resent being used as an insurance policy in this manner.

There is a famous case which illustrates another abuse. A talented television personality was forced to pay what he felt was an exorbitant amount of alimony to his ex-wife. He thereupon decided to quit show business. He took a menial, low-paying position and went back to court asking that his alimony payments be reduced. The judge refused, reasoning that a man's liability is based upon his real earning potential, not his actual paycheck. Unfortunately, the reverse is not true. It is the rare judge who will order an intelligent and capable woman into the labor market and make her work to her fullest potential. The woman is given a choice: she may remain home or go out to work. The man has no such choice.

Alimony has important tax consequences. It is a tax deduction to the giver and is taxable income to the recipient. Child support, on the other hand, is not tax deductible. Therefore, it is to a man's advantage to pay some of the child support in the form of alimony.

Inflation has a great impact on alimony. High inflation rates, such as experienced during the last several years, have the effect of reducing the alimony burden on the payer. In turn, the buying power of the recipient is reduced. A few courts write escalator clauses into alimony orders. The trouble is, the man may be caught in the middle, since his real wages may not keep up with inflation.

Some men and women would like to see alimony eliminated altogether. They believe marriage should be a "pay-as-you-go" arrangement, rather than a system where a debt is payable as alimony after divorce. If one partner wishes to put the other through school while foregoing his or her own career, or if one spouse wishes to work fourteen hours a day so the other may live a life of leisure, then they both have received the benefits of doing what makes them happy. There are no debts built up, since the choice was voluntary. Upon dissolution of the marriage, each spouse walks away knowing he has been paid in full.

On the other hand, some people believe that if one partner stays home to raise the children, and this is a mutually agreeable choice, then that partner, upon dissolution of the marriage, is entitled to what is now being called "rehabilitation." That is, it is agreed that the spouse will receive alimony for a few years until that person is able to go back into the labor market. Whichever course of action is taken, the couple should discuss the matter thoroughly and arrive at a mutually acceptable agreement.

One of the most destructive aspects of alimony is that couples are tied together long after their emotional commitments have died. Courts and society should avoid entrapping our young people into dependency relationships.

Each partner should be encouraged to be an individual and to strive for his or her maximum potential.

Financial Declarations

Courts use written financial declarations to help them establish the amount of child support and alimony. These are frequently padded and the amounts listed do not reflect reality. The adversary system forces litigants to hide income, bury assets, or resort to subterfuge. Some women feel they are entitled to list every expense they have, plus many to which they aspire. The man may inflate his living expenses in order to reduce his child support or alimony payments.

The reverse of the male who exaggerates his expenses is the one who understates them. Some men are so guilt ridden, or have such low self-images, that they only feel entitled to crumbs when the financial pie is split up. They willingly agree to keep an ex-wife and children in a beautiful suburban home, while they live in a small furnished apartment. Their responsibility to their family overshadows their own personal needs.

Rational people should look at finances honestly. Both spouses should work toward establishing budgets which are fair to all parties and within the family's resources. Women who want to take their husbands to the cleaners, or men who wish to starve their ex-wives, only hurt themselves in the end.

Legal Fees

Legal fees are a substantial financial considera-tion in most divorces. In some states they are awarded on the basis of ability to pay rather than on fault. While both parties have a right to legal representation, fairness dictates that the fees be paid out of the community estate. Since many women today have substantial earnings, the practice of awarding all or most of the attorney's fees to the husband is grossly unfair.

On the more pragmatic side, there are several points to keep in mind. The tax consequences must be considered. Legal fees for handling a divorce are not tax deductible. However, fees expended in defense or protection of income are deductible, as are fees for tax advice. There-fore, the cost of obtaining a divorce can't be written off, but if there is a hassle over alimony later, those costs are deductible.

Some lawyers are willing to allow their cli-ents to pay off the bill in monthly installments. It is preferable to pay in this manner, especially if the fees are not tax deductible. In periods of high inflation you will be paying off your bills in easy dollars. In addition, your attorney may be willing to make a lump-sum settlement for less money later.

Child Support

Child-support matters take on increasing importance as millions of children become the victims of broken homes. Judges take into consideration many factors in establishing child-support awards, including the needs of the children, their ages, the ability of the parents to pay, and previous standard of living. Some courts use a table which specifies suggested amounts of child support based on these variables.

After a divorce it is often the male who is expected to shoulder the full responsibility of child support. It is almost automatic for the children to go with Mother, for she is seen as the nurturer. Equally automatic is the assumption that the bills go to Dad, for he is the provider. A few states have declared that a father and mother, rather than the father alone, have an equal responsibility to support and educate their children, taking into consideration the respective earnings or earning capacities of the parents. Hopefully, this is the wave of the future and will catch on across the country.

One of the most common complaints of responsible fathers who pay child support is that there is no accounting of how the money is spent. Indeed, there are women who receive substantial child support which is spent on their own personal needs rather than on the children. Some women view child support as an extension of their alimony. Courts should require that the recipient of child support give a full and complete accounting of how the money is spent.

The amount of child support should be based upon what it costs to raise a child in today's economy. It is not unreasonable to include cost-of-living allowances. The amount that is fixed upon should then be divided among the two parents in proportion to their incomes.

As a case in point, one father who earns $700 a month was ordered to pay $450 in alimony and child support. While it is very difficult for a family of three to live on $700 a month, if that is all that is available then it should be allocated in a reasonable manner. It is unfair for the male to be forced to provide a standard of living higher for the other members of the family than for himself.

The duration of child support depends upon the court order. Generally, child support terminates when the offspring reaches majority, usually eighteen years of age. Sometimes, however, there is a need for continuing child support after majority is reached. A dependent child in college obviously will need some ongoing support. But the reverse may also be true. As children become self-supporting or emancipated, this should be reflected in reduced child-support payments.

The case of Paul and Robin M. illustrates an inequity. At the time of the divorce, the judge ordered Paul to pay Robin $300 a month child support for Kevin, their nine-year-old son. Robin has remarried and her new husband has been very successful. Paul, on the other hand, has had financial reverses. When Robin's father died, he left a substantial amount to Robin and Kevin. Kevin's inheritance is in trust, but provides him an income of $200 a month. When Paul went back to court claiming a change of circumstances, the judge only reduced Paul's obligation by $50 a month.

Most states follow a firm policy of separating child-support obligations and visitation rights. This means men are often forced to pay child support, while their ex-wives blatantly ignore or frustrate their visitation. Many fathers pay child support regularly to post office boxes, others to families who have been brainwashed and have great hostility toward them. A lot of men are taking the position that unless they are allowed a close and continuing relationship with their children, they do not feel a financial obligation to them. The one-sided enforcement of child-support collection and the systematic exclusion of men from the lives of their children is among the very worst abuses of men's rights.

Remarriage and Second Families

Remarriage, which often produces a network of new family ties and interrelationships, can be fraught with the potential for conflicts. Financial matters become extremely complicated when partners remarry. While parents are expected to support their natural children after a divorce, the issue is not nearly so clear with respect to stepchildren. A conscientious and loving parent may be very willing to continue supporting children from a former marriage, but may have some reluctance to support stepchildren who are already receiving child support.

The lines of loving and caring become very blurred with the financial strings in a second marriage. For example, the courts consider the total family income when deciding the amount of child support. This creates some interesting and conflicting situations. A man may remarry and a judge may ask for a financial declaration specifying the incomes of the man and his new wife. Since her income is community property, she may be called upon to help support his children from a former marriage. Many men and women feel resentful at the prospect of paying child support for somebody else's child, particularly if their own ex-spouse is failing to contribute to the children's support.

Conversely, a judge may be reluctant to ask a new husband to pay for his wife's children by a former marriage. Since there are no consistent rules, we often see great inequities in this financial merry-go-round.

As a result of capricious and unclear support practices a man may find children from his first marriage living well, while those from his second are deprived. One case comes to mind where a judge ordered $400 a month child support to children from a former marriage, while the two children from the man's second marriage had to live on $200 a month. This is heartbreaking for many men, who want to see all of their children living equally well. It also tends to create jealousy and conflict among the children.

It is obvious by now that the financial aspects of relationships play as deep a role in people's lives as emotional and psychological factors. In the next chapter we will discuss property settlements and further explore the financial, legal and tax consequences of divorce.

Slicing Up the Pie

11

Next to disputes over child custody, property settlements consume more legal expenses and create more hostility than any other aspect of divorce. Property-settlement procedures vary widely from state to state. Traditionally, in states where fault is considered, it is not uncommon to award a disproportionately large share of the family's assets to the wronged party. In community-property states, it is assumed that all property acquired during marriage belongs equally to both partners.

At the roots of the community-property concept is the notion that regardless of what each spouse contributes, their efforts, though different, are equal. This means that in a divorce, each spouse is entitled to one-half of the estate built up during the marriage.

Many couples may not be aware of the consequences of this idea in practice. If a male earns all of the money and pays for all of the assets (automobiles, house, furniture, and so on), his divorcing spouse is entitled to half even though she did not earn money outside the home. In a similar way, one-half of all the wife's earnings belongs to the husband. It does not matter whose name is shown on the automobile registration, deed of trust, or any other legal document. Ownership is still fifty-fifty.

There is another kind of property which is also important, and that is separate property. Separate property is any property acquired before marriage. As long as a partner does not commingle or intermix separate property with community, it remains his or her sole property. One can also acquire separate property during a marriage through inheritance or gifts made expressly to that person. Separate property is not divided upon a divorce, since it already belongs to one or the other spouse.

All divorcing couples should have an understanding of the basic principles of property settlements. They affect matters of divorce, inheritance, insurance and taxes. No matter how acrimonious the emotional aspects of divorce may be, both partners should work toward an equitable division of all property. Wives who want to take their husbands to the cleaners or men who wish to take advantage of unknowledgeable women create many problems for themselves and their families. Fairness dictates that both partners divide commu-

nity property equally and not try to lay claim to
the other party's separate holdings.

A fair division of community property may
require the use of appraisers, accountants, and
attorneys. But such items as the family dwelling, furniture, insurance, retirement funds, and
family business should and must be disposed of
in an equitable manner. Here are some important things to consider when dividing community property.

Many people are not aware of the tax aspects
of property settlements. More than a few
spouses who thought they got fair treatment in
the settlement discovered they were ripped off
when they had to settle with the Internal Reve-
nue Service. Others find that they cannot bank
or spend their share of what at first appears to
be an equal division of property.

We have already discussed the idea of the T-
account for listing assets and distributing them
fairly. Whenever possible, assets should be
fairly evaluated prior to their distribution.
Some things, such as stocks or bonds, can be
valued with some degree of accuracy. Other
items, such as goodwill of a business, works of
art, or such sentimental things as family photo-
graphs or heirlooms, may be difficult to put a
price on. Where possible, appraisal costs, accounting fees and the like should be borne
equally by both spouses.

Pets or other belongings that cannot be valued are extremely difficult to dispose of in a di-

vorce. In one case, a Detroit couple was unwilling to give up their monthly duplicate-bridge group. After much hassle, they finally worked out a compromise in which the husband and his new wife play one month, and the ex-wife plays the next. In another instance a New York couple worked out a visitation schedule which permitted each to spend time with their collie. As one judge put it, "I try to divide the dog to get the love and attention of both."

Basic Accounting

Accountants often use some high-sounding terms to describe some very basic ideas. Most of the time we don't understand what our accountant is talking about and are too intimidated to admit it. We end up following his advice blindly without really knowing what is going on. So let's take a few moments to look at some basic accounting ideas in simple terms. These are very important to you in property settlements.

Assets. An asset is anything of worth. A home, automobile, cash in the bank, and stocks and bonds are all assets. If you owe money on a car, the car is still an asset, since you have some ownership or equity in it.

All assets are not the same. Some are liquid and some are not. A liquid asset is one that can readily be converted into cash. Stocks, bonds, treasury bills, and similar assets can easily be sold. They can be converted into spendable cash on relatively short notice.

Nonliquid assets are those which have a value, but which cannot be converted into cash so easily. A retirement plan, oil paintings, jewelry, or a family business may take months, or even years, to convert to cash. Further, it is extremely difficult to assess how much money will be realized until the item is actually sold.

It is usually better to have liquid assets than nonliquid. This is because you can convert them into spendable cash of a relatively predictable amount in short order. The failure to consider liquidity has created some grossly unfair property settlements.

Peter L. accepted his pension plan, life-insurance equity, and the family business as his share of the settlement. His wife got cash and the family home. On the surface there was an equal division of property. But Peter hadn't considered liquidity. While he got half the assets, he soon found he couldn't spend them. A year after the divorce his ex-wife sold the house and bought a condominium. She had a lot of cash left over and took an extended vacation with her new boyfriend. Peter, on the other hand, could not cash in his life insurance because the judge ordered it kept in force. His pension plan would not come due for eleven years. The business itself enabled him to earn a living as long as he worked, but the $30,000 of goodwill wasn't spendable. One year after the divorce

Peter was living in a furnished apartment, barely able to make both ends meet.

Liabilities. Liabilities are debts, money owed to others, or unpaid bills. If you owe money on a car, have unpaid charge accounts, or are paying off creditors, you have liabilities.

Liabilities incurred during a marriage should be viewed as community obligations. The responsibility for paying off these debts should be distributed equally between the spouses. If you are assigned the debts, then you should also receive an additional offsetting asset.

Present value of the dollar. Present value of the dollar is based on the concept that a bird in the hand is worth two in the bush. Most people would prefer to receive money today rather than at a later date. Money has time value in that it is worth more to you now than later. Accountants say that the present value of future money is the amount that an informed investor would be willing to pay today to receive it. Present value is figured on the length of time you will have to wait to get the money, the rate of return, and the amount of the future payment.

In simple terms, a note for $10,000 payable in five years at eight percent is of less value to you than $10,000 now. Accountants use tables which tell them the present value of any dollar amount, given the length of time and the rate of return. The present value is always less than the future amount due. Whenever assets are distributed, they should be based upon their present value, which can be determined by an accountant.

Uncle Sam's Share

Federal and state taxes must be considered in property settlements. An equal division of property that is co-owned by a husband and wife is not taxable. The tax man says that a nontaxable exchange takes place when a couple divides community property equally. So if you get the house and she gets the furniture and car, it is not treated as a sale. It does not matter that the car has declined in value while the house has doubled in worth. As long as there is an equal division and the items are not sold but only split up, no taxes are due.

A different situation occurs when one party sells an asset at a later date. If you buy an asset, hold it for some length of time, and sell it for more than you paid, then you incur a capital-gains tax liability. The actual tax due is based upon what you paid (your basis) versus what you sold it for. Your accountant will help you figure the actual amount of money due.

The point is, this future tax liability should be taken into consideration when you prepare your settlement. Suppose you wind up with the house, and its market value is $100,000. If you sell it and have to pay $10,000 capital-gains tax, then you are actually receiving an asset worth $90,000. In a similar way, if you get a $100,000 retirement fund and have to pay $30,000 of income tax, then the asset is worth only $70,000. It is imperative that you be aware of the true net worth of all assets.

A House Is More Than a Home

We have already dealt with the intrinsic value of the family home, and in particular the need to be aware of capital-gains taxes which may be due. Now let's turn to the emotional and psychological side of disposing of the house.

The person who winds up with the family home has some real advantages. If you are lucky enough to get the house, you will probably find that the children will want to stay in their familiar surroundings. Usually the pets stay with the kids and the house also. You have a lot of bargaining advantages and can likely ask for and receive the furniture as well.

The house is a relatively liquid asset which is rising at or above the rate of inflation. You are paying off a loan which you may not be able to qualify for today and which you probably got at a substantially lower interest rate than is available today. So if you do nothing more than stay in the house, you're ahead.

The months you spent searching for the house, the cost of obtaining the loan, and the hours spent ordering and installing utilities should not be underrated. You may not realize what is involved till you buy another house. There are other small, comforting advantages such as not having to change your address on your drivers license, library card or credit cards. You'll probably even get to keep the remainder of your magazine subscriptions.

There is security in staying on your home ground during times of crisis. The person who gets the house picks up a lot of fringe benefits.

But there are some liabilities. Capital gains has already been discussed. There are some less obvious problems that have nothing to do with money. If you have lived in the house as a couple for any length of time, it is filled with memories. All the good times are there, as are the bad times at the end. The house is a constant reminder of the fighting, bickering and arguments. You may wind up with the house, but also with a crippling emotional burden.

Economists tell us it makes good financial sense to leverage your money. If you have lived in the house for many years, you probably have a substantial amount of equity in the property. There is a lot of money that isn't working for you. If you sell the house, and both spouses reinvest in new properties, you will be better off emotionally and financially.

The distribution of furniture and household belongings is another underrated item in property settlements. Few judges and too few divorcing men recognize just how much is involved in replacing furniture. The time and effort expended in choosing not only large pieces of furniture, but accessories, are not taken into consideration. It is easy to overlook such items as linens, towels, silverware, dishes, crystal, china, serving pieces, and other household goods.

The easiest and fairest way to divide up furniture and household items is with a "pick list." List all items and put a mutually agreed upon value on each. Toss a coin to determine who gets first choice. Then alternately make one selection each from the list. This divides things reasonably and shifts the burden for acquiring new items equally between spouses. After the list has been run through, the partners may then make trades.

Sometimes there are items, such as cameras, stamp or coin collections, or jewelry, which are highly desired by one partner. Some spouses use this as a weapon. They have the item appraised at an unrealistically high value, knowing it will be sought after. This is unfair and creates a hostile atmosphere which will affect the settlement of other issues.

Insurance and Pension Plans

Some types of insurance policies, including those which have been in force for many years, may have substantial cash value. In some settlements couples opt to cash in the policies and

split the proceeds. However, some judges order
policies to be kept in force and then award the
cash value to the husband. This is an unjust
practice in that the man receives nonspendable
dollars. Not only that, he also has to keep paying the premiums. If the insurance policy is
given to one party with orders to keep it in
force, this should be offset by a similar nonliquid or nonspendable asset on the other side.

Many spouses contribute to retirement funds
or pension plans during their marriage. This is
a community asset but may be difficult to divide equally. Some pension plans contain vested and nonvested funds. A vested fund can be
withdrawn by the employee upon termination
with the company. Some employers do not vest
their contribution until the employee has spent
ten years with the firm. If he leaves before ten
years, he loses any contribution that the employer makes to the fund. If the employee remains for ten years, the employer's contribution then goes to him when he leaves or retires.

Many judges will award the husband the pension fund without considering how much of it
is vested. He may give the wife cash in the
bank or real estate as an offset. Some men
don't remain with the company long enough to
receive the employer's contribution. Since men
have shorter life expectancies than women,
they may not live long enough to see any of the
money. Accountants can reduce retirement
funds to present value. This is the amount that
should be used in the settlement.

Another solution is to divide the pension-plan proceeds only when they are payable. Some plans are kept in force after a divorce and include further payments out of separate property. Accountants have a formula to compensate for these additional contributions.

Many profit-sharing and corporate retirement plans, as well as individual plans, are based upon deferred taxation. This means the individual may place substantial funds in these plans and not pay taxes until they are withdrawn. These funds may look substantial until you consider the tax implications.

Consider the case of Lloyd and Amy G. During their marriage they opened a Keough account in Lloyd's name, because he was self-employed. Over the years, fifteen percent of his income was put into this fund and no taxes were paid on the money. When they divorced, the fund of over $100,000 was given to Lloyd, while Amy was given cash and the house. Later Lloyd found that if he were to draw money out of the Keough plan before retirement age, he would have to pay a ten percent penalty plus income tax. The $100,000 shrank to a little over $50,000.

Goodwill and Bad Feelings

Goodwill is the economic value assigned to the reputation and clientele of a business. It is sometimes called "key money." This is above and beyond the physical assets of the business. For example, a long-established business may have a substantial amount of goodwill associated with it. If the owner chose to sell it, he might be able to get $50,000 for the equipment, fixtures and other tangible assets. However, a prospective buyer may also be willing to pay an additional $20,000 just for the key. This is because it may cost a new proprietor $20,000 in promotion and advertising to build up the stream of customers which readily come into the store.

Inflated or unrealistic goodwill is sometimes used as a means of balancing a property settlement. A wife may be given the lion's share of the property and then offset the amount by attributing it to goodwill. You cannot spend goodwill, you cannot pay rent, alimony or child support with it.

Goodwill is very difficult to assess. Legal, medical and accounting practices consist mainly of clients who use the service because of the personality, experience or knowledge of the practitioner. In their absence, there is virtually no goodwill, since the individual is the practice. It is specifically because goodwill is hard to pin down that it is used by judges as an easy out in balancing property settlements.

Accounts receivable is another factor which must be considered when valuing a business. Accounts receivable is the money owed to a business by customers who have purchased goods or services on credit. It may be an important part of the property settlement because it is community property. A portion of accounts receivable is usually uncollectible. It is not fair to give the spouse who receives the business the accounts receivable at full value without considering what percentage is never going to be collected. An accountant who is experienced in valuing accounts receivable can compute their estimated worth with some degree of accuracy.

Balancing the Scales

It sometimes happens that community property cannot be divided exactly down the middle. This is most common when there is a large single asset such as a home or a business which both parties agree should not be sold. It is common practice to give one party a note to offset the value of the item.

The best way to equalize these situations is to see that all major assets are fairly evaluated and equally distributed on the basis of current value and liquidity. If the male agrees voluntarily to take a note, the note should be discounted to reflect its true value. The interest rate should be whatever is current, and the note should be for a reasonable length of time. The note should be paid in full if the asset is sold.

Phantom Debts

There is a difficult philosophical issue involved in establishing an economic value on education, professional degrees, and personal growth achieved during a marriage. Some people argue that these things are much like physical assets. They were obtained at an economic cost, and the partner who has the asset must reimburse the other in kind after divorce.

As an example, Doreen B. took care of the kids and kept them quiet while her husband Sheldon studied for his CPA degree. During the lean years she lived on a meager budget while he studied late into the night, since he had to support the family during the day. After Sheldon passed the CPA exam, his practice grew rapidly. He loved his work and spent long hours at it. Their lifestyle reflected his financial success, and for twenty years they mutually enjoyed all the fruits of his hard work. They had a full-time maid, traveled extensively, and Doreen spent her time at luncheons and shopping while he was at work.

When the divorce occurred, Doreen's attorney demanded that Sheldon continue to provide her with the same lifestyle she had been accustomed to for the last twenty years. The lawyer also asked that Sheldon pay for Doreen's education while she obtained a degree as a psychologist. Sheldon was asked to support Doreen to the Ph.D. level.

The attorney's rationale for these demands

was that since Sheldon had earned his degree during the marriage, Doreen was entitled to similar schooling. This is a specious argument. It overlooks several fundamental points.

Sheldon supported the family while he was going to school. He also gave up his leisure time to study, at great personal sacrifice. He provided a great measure of luxury to his wife during the twenty years after he graduated. Sheldon suggested many times during the marriage that Doreen go to school, since she was intellectually gifted. She chose a course of personal indulgence and did not develop her potential. Sheldon's debt was paid by the gift of twenty years of luxurious living.

Much of this problem will remedy itself because of the attitudes of the new generation. There are now more women attending higher-education institutions than males. These women are asking for, and deserve, their place in society and an equal opportunity for professional training and careers.

Closing the Door Gently

12

Ron and Sheila K. spent two years and $40,000 before their divorce battle was over. Hostility was rampant as they fought bitterly over custody and visitation matters. Their three children suffered because of their anger.

In desperation they decided to go to a divorce mediator. After eight sessions, and for less than $500, they were able to reach an agreement without returning to court.

"It was just awful," recalls Sheila. "Our anger was terribly destructive and the courtroom atmosphere only made things worse. But when we met with the mediator, the whole thing made more sense. She took an insane atmosphere and made it sane."

Society is fraught with conflict-producing situations. None are treated with less caring and skill than divorce settlements. There are positive alternatives to knockdown, drag-out fights and courtroom showdowns. People are finding that conciliation courts, mediation, arbitration, and post-divorce counseling are less painful methods of settling difficult domestic matters.

There are three distinct stages in relationships where conflict resolution and outside intervention may be needed. If a couple is experiencing marital problems, they may need counseling, therapy, or conciliation services as a means of resolving differences. If a divorce or separation becomes inevitable, the couple may call upon therapists, counselors, conciliators, mediators, or arbitrators. After a divorce or dissolution, the couple may still require help to resolve conflicts related to custody, visitation, remarriage, stepparenting, and other conflict-producing situations.

Many people are unaware of the services in their communities which can help them during these three critical phases of a relationship. Even when people know these services exist, they don't know how to use them effectively. Nonjudicial conflict-resolving services are not panaceas. But they do offer a less expensive, quicker, and often less emotionally draining means of solving problems.

Patching Things Up

A troubled marriage can sometimes be improved with the aid of a skilled family therapist, conciliator, social worker, or other professional. The intent of conciliation is to save a relationship through identification of problems and change of behavior. Skilled therapists will help find nondestructive ways of coping with anger and hostility. Therapy assists individuals or families in crisis. A good therapist identifies real problems and does not merely treat symptoms. The counselor seeks to help family members deal with each other in a nonmanipulative way, avoiding game playing and stressing the value and effectiveness of open and healthy communication.

There are various agencies that can be called upon to help a troubled family. Churches, social-service agencies, and conciliation courts provide individual and family therapy sessions. Counseling and one-on-one or group therapy help individuals deal with sexual adjustments, communication problems, discipline, in-law or money-related issues.

When the Marriage Is Over

A day may come when a couple realizes that a relationship can't be saved, that they have reached the end of the line and there is no turning back. Divorce may be the only answer. But the process is fraught with conflict and crisis. It is during these critical times that experienced professionals can help wind down the relationship in the least destructive way.

This is when people need help dealing with

the feelings of alienation, loneliness, fear and anxiety which are generated when a relationship dies. Counselors can help establish new identities for the spouses, separate and apart from each other. But there is only so much that they can do. Dissolution sometimes involves bitter disputes over property, money, custody, or other legal matters. There are times when a skilled conciliator or mediator is better able to resolve these conflicts than a mental-health professional.

Mediators or conciliators do not deal with emotional and psychological problems, as the therapist does. They are expert in the art of negotiation, trading, compromise, and settlement. Their tools are offers, counteroffers, trading points and balance sheets. They deal with the economic realities of disengaging the parties.

A mediator, using many of the same tools of the labor negotiator who must deal with contested emotional issues, relies upon personal influence and persuasion to steer couples away from fault finding and onto realistic settlements. Their job is to identify key bargaining issues. Legal advice is left to the attorneys and psychological aid to the therapists.

Agencies for Conflict Resolution

There are two important agencies, of which divorcing spouses should be aware, that provide mental-health professionals or skilled mediators in divorce situations. Conciliation courts are staffed by social workers, counselors, psychologists, and psychiatrists. They focus on the mental-health aspect of conflict resolution. The American Arbitration Association draws heavily upon trained domestic-relations attorneys, clergymen, and social workers. They stress mediation and arbitration. It is important to know how each of these services can be used in resolving heated divorce disputes.

The Conciliation Court

Many states have instituted special departments in their family-law courts to provide counseling and mediation. These are called conciliation courts and are empowered to conduct investigations and evaluations, and to make recommendations.

Their staff, usually composed of behavioral scientists, is trained to deal with a wide range of marriage and family problems. They work out custody and visitation agreements and assist in crisis marriage and divorce counseling. Some deal with premarital counseling and even post-divorce problems.

One of the problems faced by the conciliation court is its name and identity. Too often it is associated only with patching up broken marriages. This is only one small part of their services, and people should not be put off by the name.

Los Angeles County serves as a good example

of how the conciliation court is used effectively. All contested custody and visitation matters are remanded there before they can be heard by a judge. The proceedings of the conciliation conference are confidential. The staff may issue a report and make recommendations to the judge. In going about their work, the staff may interview family members and conduct psychological tests and evaluations.

Couples who have used conciliation-court services often speak very highly of them. They tell us they foster a conciliatory attitude between spouses which enables them to work out acceptable agreements. Many couples reluctantly go to conciliation court, confident that it won't work. They come away praising the understanding and help they obtain there.

Others complain that the conciliation court's staff is biased against fathers or is unwilling to conduct in-depth investigations. On balance, however, the court provides positive services which should be taken advantage of before engaging in a hostile courtroom battle.

The American Arbitration Association

The American Arbitration Association is a nonprofit, public-service organization dedicated to resolving disputes of all kinds. They provide conciliation, mediation, arbitration, and other voluntary means of breaking impasses. The AAA maintains a family-dispute services section which is available to individuals or families. They assist in drafting separation agreements and in helping parties negotiate settlements. They also render binding decisions when parties cannot agree. The AAA provides a private, dignified, and convenient means of conflict resolution, and is not intended to give legal advice.

The AAA's main office is 140 W. 51st Street, New York, New York 10020. They maintain regional offices in many major cities across the country.

There is a distinct difference between mediation and arbitration. Mediators do not have decision-making power. They assist couples in reaching their own agreement. Arbitrators have the power to render binding decisions.

The principal tool mediators use is negotiation. They stress alternatives and compromise. They help parties organize trading points and counterproposals. They establish ground rules for bargaining. Mediation provides an atmosphere in which one can give in without losing face. At the root of the mediation process is the idea that the parties work out their own solution. The mediator has no conclusive power, but works in an objective way suggesting areas for settlement and avoiding impossible situations.

With the best efforts, some conflicts cannot be resolved through counseling or mediation. It is sometimes necessary for couples to turn to arbitration. In his most basic function a judge is an arbitrator. A judge has conclusive power over the parties and makes the decisions. However, the judicial process is bound by legal technicalities and procedures. The reliance upon a judge as the ultimate decision maker is a slow, costly means of resolving an impasse.

The AAA has a Panel of Marital Arbitrators which is composed of domestic-relations attorneys, clergymen, social workers, and others with special knowledge of the field. There is an administrative fee of $100. Some arbitrators serve without fee, while others charge by the hour.

Parties initiate arbitration by contacting AAA and stating that their marriage is irretrievably broken. They must agree to incorporate the arbitrator's decision in the separation agreement and to abide by it. The couple must also promise not to transfer, encumber or conceal property, or remove children from the jurisdiction.

The arbitrator holds a conference with the parties. They state areas of mutual agreement and identify unresolved issues. If the parties cannot agree on the disposition of property, the arbitrator will decide on an equitable apportionment of assets. The arbitrator may determine appropriate maintenance for either spouse. In establishing the amount of maintenance, the arbitrator ignores fault, and instead looks to the individual's personal needs, the time necessary to acquire education and training, age, living standards, and so forth.

The arbitrator may also assist in determining the amount of child support where the parties cannot agree. Resources of the child and the parents are considered, as are standard of living and other factors. Sometimes the parties cannot agree with respect to custody and visitation rights. In these instances, the arbitrator will consider the wishes of the parents and the child, the home, school, and other factors, and render a binding decision.

This may sound like the same process which is conducted in a courtroom, simply substituting an arbitrator for a judge. However, there are several significant differences. The arbitrator is not bound by the same rules of evidence and procedures as the judge. It is not an adversary arena. The arbitrator may be trained in behavioral sciences and specialize in matters of family-conflict resolution.

Since attorneys are not involved, costs are substantially lower than a court proceeding. The decision may be reached much more quickly, usually within thirty days of the end of the proceedings.

The work of the AAA is a big step in the right direction. Arbitration should be expanded to replace a substantial amount of the workload now handled by the courts. It should become a major function of our system of dispensing family-law justice.

Post-Divorce Conflicts

Hostility, anger and heartache may exist long after the legal divorce is complete. These destructive forces may interfere with relationships with both the opposite sex and with one's children. In such cases there is frequently a need for post-divorce conflict resolution.

Even though the economic, legal, and property matters are disposed of, a couple may remain emotionally tied together. Post-divorce counseling has proven to be an excellent means of completing the divorce. If there are children, there may be a continuing need for contact. Post-divorce counseling aids divorced couples to communicate and helps to diffuse potentially explosive confrontations.

There is often a great increase in hostility between divorced people when one partner decides to remarry. Remarriage often disrupts a stable situation and may create bitterness and anger. Post-divorce counseling deals with these problems.

Many couples who accept the need for marital counseling and therapy fail to recognize its importance after divorce. They see counseling as a tool for resolving conflicts within their marriage, or during the divorce, and do not realize that the post-divorce benefits may be even greater.

Post-divorce counseling is useful in reworking custody arrangements as children grow older, or as family economic conditions change. Some counselors are beginning to specialize in post-divorce services. They have become expert in dealing with the problems of remarriage, joint-custody agreements, and stepparenting.

Evaluating the Experts

The inexperienced person who turns to a therapist for help may be bewildered by the variety of approaches used. There are psychiatrists, psychologists, Masters of Social Work (MSW's), Marriage and Family Counselors (MFC's), social workers, sex therapists, and many others. Each of these categories has sub-categories, and all of them have differing views and approaches.

Some therapists delve into the patient's early childhood, others deal only with what is happening now. Some give advice, others just listen. Some prescribe drugs, others exercises. There are therapists who rely on primal screams, hug therapy, and sexual surrogates. College degrees, personal experience, or professional trappings do not in themselves assure quality counseling.

Sometimes people in need of help will refuse to turn to professionals and instead seek the advice of a close friend or neighbor. There are times in life when all that is needed to solve a problem is a warm, supportive listener. In general, though, it is better to seek the assistance of someone who has been trained in the behavioral sciences.

Some therapists rely heavily upon directive therapy while others use nondirective methods. The nondirective therapist may spend many hours with a client, encouraging him or her to reveal inner feelings and emotions. There is no attempt to make value judgments or give advice. For many people this course works. They are able to frame their own solutions to problems, with the therapist acting only as a facilitator.

For other people, a more directive approach works better. Many couples need advice, concrete guidelines and someone to help them understand their conduct and behavior. For these individuals advice from the therapist is more helpful than hours of nonjudgmental listening.

Successful therapy is characterized by certain essential elements. Here are some things to look for:

1. Any treatment program should result in improved behavior. It should manifest itself in better relations with your spouse, ex-spouse, family, or others with whom you interact.

2. Therapy should help the person express emotions, fears, and confusions. It should help the individual open up to the outside world.

3. A good therapist will help a person understand and take responsibility for his or her behavior.

4. Therapy should encourage independence. It should help the individual attain the tools to solve his or her own problems.

5. There should be observable results in a reasonable length of time. Some problems may take years to work out, but there should be some indications of progress along the way. People should not hesitate to change therapists if they feel they are not being helped.

6. Be wary of therapists who solve all problems with pills. There are times when medication is indicated, but be careful of simply treating symptoms. It's an easy way out, but not a satisfactory solution for the long run.

7. Therapy can only be successful if it is directed at the proper person or persons. Sometimes both spouses need to be in treatment, and often the whole family should be involved.

8. There is no one best method of treatment for all problems. Good therapy is eclectic and should be tailored to the individual's needs and situation.

Some problems are best solved without therapists. It is important to use the appropriate problem solver. An attorney is not a social worker or therapist, and a therapist cannot solve legal problems. Other problems are best solved through mediation and arbitration. Divorce and its attendant problems may necessitate the use of several dissimilar helping persons, each dealing with a different phase of the problem.

Happy Again

13

The kids giggled as they watched television. Ted sat on the couch with his arm around his wife Rita. "How pleasant things are," he thought. "The kids are doing better in school, business has picked up, and the house is almost completely furnished." As he looked at his family, a wave of happiness washed over Ted. Then suddenly a twinge of pain intruded into his thoughts as he was swept back to that rainy evening five years ago.

Ted and his former wife Norma had had a terrible fight. It was an ugly scene. He had slammed the door in rage and stalked out. He knew he would never forget the hours spent looking for a motel room late at night. The memories were still sharp and distressing, even five years later. Life was so hopeless then, and he was convinced it would never be better.

Ted was brought back to the present as Rita whispered in his ear, "Why don't we trade weekends with Norma and go to Uncle Brad's cabin, just the two of us?"

"That's a great idea, honey," Ted replied. "You know, Norma really did me a favor, even though I couldn't appreciate it at the time. No one could have made me believe five years ago that I would ever be happy again."

Researchers tell us that most people remarry and go on to build normal, healthy relationships and productive lives. They also tell us that second marriages are usually happier than first marriages.

Couples who marry young often find that many changes take place over the years. The things they look for in a partner when they are young are not the same things they want when they are older and wiser. The world is full of good people in bad marriages. Mismatching is one of the biggest causes of divorce. Two emotionally healthy and stable individuals may end up with a failed marriage. There are many subtle but extremely important elements that make for compatibility.

Years ago the theory was that opposites attracted each other, and this was assumed to make for a good match. While it may be true that people with opposing views, physical needs or other characteristics are drawn to each other, their union does not usually create a fulfilling relationship. In fact, quite the contrary. Sound marriages should be built upon similarities and compatibility. Differences that do not seem important at the beginning of a relationship, magnify with time. When the person who loves to dance marries a nondancer; when the warm, hugging type marries the cold, untouchable person; when the athlete marries the delicate orchid; then the seeds of dissension and divorce are planted at the moment they walk to the altar.

Everyone has an internal clock. Some people come awake at night. Others function best during the day. Some are compulsively neat while others are comfortable in a disorderly and disheveled environment. The need for touching and cuddling also varies with the individual. There is nothing inherently wrong with these human characteristics. But the elements of marital disaster are present when people are mismatched. Partners become resentful when they cannot share their pleasures with their mate. They begin to do things alone or with friends, and soon find themselves living separate lives.

When choosing a new mate, people rarely repeat this mistake. They tend to choose partners who share their interests and pleasures.

Patterns of Divorce

Isolina Ricci, a teacher and counselor, has described the evolution of families moving through the divorce cycle. Ricci says divorce and reconstruction follow a familiar, seven-stage pattern. The first stage consists of a two-parent household where trust and respect exist. Trouble and discord develop during the second stage. In the third stage the two-parent household shows signs of cracking under severe difficulties and there is a threat of separation.

The household breaks apart in the fourth stage. The shocked and estranged partners are now in two separate residences. This is a period of marital dysfunction and partners feel demoralized. In the fifth stage two one-parent households become established. There is still anger and hostility which must be resolved.

Order and balance emerge in the sixth stage in both households. Children adjust to new neighborhoods, schools and the custody schedule. By the last stage, two households have emerged, each as a separate, healthy entity. Love, companionship, and respect are once more present.

The next piece of the pattern falls into place when the parties remarry. An extended family develops, new children may be born, and a complex of new relationships emerges. There are stepchildren, stepparents, ex-grandparents, aunts and uncles, and others who now play a part in a new and broader family structure.

The transition is not easy. Both men and women experience stress at this time. The process of meeting a new partner and building a new relationship may be frustrating, or it may be exciting and fulfilling. The breakup and re-construction may occur gradually over many years, or it may take place suddenly with explosive force.

Suddenly Single

Many separated and divorced men and women experience the shock of being thrown into to-day's singles world. People who have come out of a long marriage may have difficulty coping with the standards and mores of the 1980's. The "future shock" they experience is often devastating.

Many men and women describe their reentry into the singles world in mixed terms. For some, there is a feeling of being in limbo. They live for the moment. They can't bear to remember the past and they are unable to make plans for the future. The habit of being married is hard to shake. It may persist for months or even years after a divorce. It is not uncommon for a newly separated man to start phoning his home when he is running late, only to realize that there is no one to call.

People who are thrust into the singles world complain of feelings of failure or inadequacy. Some harbor a hostility for their former spouses which colors their new relationships. They fear becoming two-time losers and avoid new attachments for fear of being hurt again.

For the male, coping with being alone again has its unique and traumatizing aspects. Some men throw themselves into an endless round of one-night stands or short-term relationships, hoping to reestablish their self-worth. Others are afraid to venture out for fear of rejection. There are men who, dispossessed of their households, find they have difficulty occupying their time. There is no lawn to mow or leaky faucet to fix. Many men must learn to do the most basic of household chores. Learning to run a load of wash or knowing when to remove a shirt from the dryer often proves to be an anxiety-provoking experience. A man may spend his day making multimillion-dollar real-estate deals, and then go home and find he is unable to handle shopping for a loaf of bread or a quart of milk.

The experience of becoming newly single is no less draining on the female. Women also experience many of the same feelings as men. If they are the rejected party, they sometimes wish to strike back at all men. Some women will tease, frustrate or deceive the men they meet. A woman whose long marriage has ended finds herself in an unfamiliar world filled with confident young college girls and successful career women. The competition may be overwhelming.

Once they are over the initial reentry trauma, however, many men and women welcome their second chance at life. They find it exciting to meet new partners, explore new sexual experi-

ences, new places, new foods and new lifestyles. Divorce often forces a valuable self-
assessment. Many men and women come out of
this period with greater understanding, self-respect and confidence. They are not only able to
cope with life, but can now direct and guide
their own destinies.

Meeting new people often creates a fresh self-
image. A woman may discover she is more attractive than her former husband found her to
be. A man often learns that the things his ex-
wife didn't like are attractive to a new woman.

Sometimes selling the house and moving to
an apartment relieves a lot of pressure. For
some men the freedom from the burden of a
spouse allows them the opportunity to do
things they couldn't do before. They can
change jobs, move to a new city, go to school, or
take chances. The period between marriages
can be a positive time of assessment, reconstruction and personal growth.

Starting Over

The frenzied running from one affair to another and the excitement of meeting new
people soon give way to a need for the continuity of a deeper relationship. Before long
many people find themselves looking for someone to love and share their lives with.

Loving relationships represent an investment

of yourself in someone else's life. The pairing
process is one of growth and evolution. It begins with a look or a casual touch, and grows
as people learn more about each other and
share common experiences. Soon the couple become as heavily invested in each other as they
were in their former partners.

This is the reverse of separation and divorce,
where there is a gradual phasing out of concern
and interest for another human being. Couples
are often unaware of the subtle and almost im-
perceptible changes taking place in their lives.
Even when the break comes abruptly and without warning, the foundation may have been
laid over many years. In a similar way, the
foundation for building a new relationship is
laid stone by stone.

Eventually most couples want to make their
families and the world aware of the depth of
their new commitment. The second marriage
often brings a new level of happiness and stability to many men. However, remarriage
brings with it a host of emotional, economic
and legal complexities.

Money is high on the list of trouble makers in
a second marriage. When a young couple marries for the first time, they assemble a community estate. They work together to build a home
and financial security. There is one common
pot into which everything is thrown. There is
no "his"or "hers" since everything is "theirs."

In a new marriage there are several economic
pots. Either or both partners may have substan-

tial separate assets which they wish to preserve as separate property. At the same time they want to build a new common estate. It is natural for many people to want to keep their share of an estate from a former marriage so that they may pass it on to their natural children. Thus, the former economic simplicity is replaced by a complex set of equities. It is no easy matter to maintain fairness and balance between the new spouse and the children or other relatives of a former marriage.

Money, or the lack of it, creates jealousy and hostility. It can be very troubling to a man of moderate means who marries a well-to-do woman. His macho inculturation puts him in the impossible bind of feeling he has to carry the financial load himself. If the family lives only on his income, they have to do without a lot of luxuries they have been accustomed to. But if they live on her money, he feels unimportant and unnecessary.

Conversely, if a woman with limited assets marries a man of means, there is a different set of problems. She often feels hurt by his desire to preserve his estate for his children. She may also resent his ability to buy luxuries for himself which she cannot afford. At the same time, his children are angry when he spends money on his new wife, feeling that it lessens their inheritance.

The fact that both partners are equally well-to-do does not ensure a lack of problems. When Jan and Eric C. were married their marriage ran into trouble almost immediately. Both had a substantial estate from former marriages. Yet Jan expected Eric to pay all their expenses out of his funds, leaving hers intact. Eric felt he was being taken advantage of and his children considered themselves cheated.

Then there are the problems Vicky and Hal F. are facing. Both walked away from their former marriages virtually penniless, and Hal is saddled with high alimony and child-support payments. They find their paychecks don't stretch enough to cover their basic necessities, and luxuries are out of the question. Hal is particularly distressed by the fact that his new family is not living as well as the children from his former marriage.

Vicky is extremely upset because she believes she is working to subsidize Hal's ex-wife and children. She has reason to feel this way, since Hal's child-support payments have been raised due to her income.

Another major problem remarried couples face is dealing with children. Both partners usually have children from a previous marriage. Sometimes they have children together, also. Stepchildren often resent stepparents, and vice versa. Or the children may accept the stepparents but dislike each other. A husband or wife can be jealous when his or her spouse is overly attentive to the children. The potential for conflict is enormous and unending.

Arline J. was once George J.'s stepdaughter. When she came home to her mother after her divorce, Arline fell in love with her mother's new husband. George reciprocated the feeling and left his wife to marry Arline. Ellen, George's ex-wife and Arline's mother, is now bitterly hostile toward both her daughter and her ex-husband.

Arnie and Beth V. have a different problem. They both had fourteen-year-old children from previous marriages, and the children took an instant dislike to each other. Arnie and Beth cannot leave the children alone because they fight constantly. The boys are too old for a baby-sitter, and Arnie and Beth are unable to leave home. If Arnie overreacts and disciplines Beth's son, Beth gets upset. And Arnie becomes angry when Beth complains about his son. When Arnie disciplines his son, the boy claims Arnie is favoring Beth's son. Arnie and Beth love each other, are well matched, and when they are able to steal some time alone, get along well. But the children are having a greatly adverse effect on their relationship.

A divorce may make new friends out of old acquaintances and turn old friends into strangers. Some people who were simply acquaintances before the divorce hit it off better with the new spouse and become close friends. Others drop both members of a divorcing couple for any number of reasons.

There are those who would like to remain friendly with both parties. Many people find they feel a kinship with new couples who also have been divorced and remarried. They have a common bond and understand the problems. They usually are not judgmental as some ex-friends are.

Relationships with ex-in-laws must also be dealt with, inasmuch as they are still the children's grandparents, aunts and uncles. A rift between a couple should not necessarily mean an estrangement with in-laws. Many men have become almost second sons to their in-laws and have been treated with love and kindness.

Children want both parents to attend weddings, bar mitzvahs, and graduations. An unmarried ex-spouse sometimes feels uncomfortable in the presence of the new spouse. Meetings at family gatherings can generate a lot of tension. Much tact is needed at these times.

When You Remarry

The reader may think that with all of these problems, happiness is difficult to attain in a second marriage. If not properly dealt with these problems can sow the seeds of another divorce. It may take professional help, or a deep understanding and caring on the part of the wives, to help men deal with the inevitable conflicts generated by their new marriages. But there are ways to minimize these problems.

Here are some practical hints and suggestions which can help with the day-to-day problems encountered when people remarry.

1. Recognize that money problems are inevitable, and solutions need to be carefully thought out. Trouble can be avoided by preparing an equitable prenuptial agreement. A good set of written records will go a long way toward reducing conflicts. For example, prepare a detailed list of all separate property. Consult an attorney or an accountant and discuss how trusts can be set up that will protect both the spouses and the children.

If you feel you are being taken advantage of, bring your feelings out in the open. Perhaps post-divorce counseling can help solve the problems.

2. Play your own unique role in the lives of your stepchildren. Divorce creates stepparents, it does not eliminate natural parents. Be a friend rather than a surrogate parent. Don't talk against the natural parent, either directly or by innuendo. Avoid competing with the natural parent for the child's attention and favor. It is destructive to play favorites, or to play one child against the other.

Discipline is a crucial area of conflict. Discuss problems without the children present and agree on how to handle various situations. A couple should always be consistent in their discipline decisions and should not undermine each other. Don't allow problems with the children to interfere in your new relationship. If problems appear to be unmanageable, seek outside help.

3. Develop new friends based on your new union. Many couples discover there is a fresh chemistry which attracts a different set of friends. Avoid putting people who wish to maintain friendships with both divorcing spouses into an either/or situation. Don't use them as a dumping ground for bitterness against your former spouse.

4. Encourage children to maintain an ongoing relationship with grandparents, aunts, uncles and other family members of your former marriage, but don't expect to be included. There will be times when you will be expected to interact with your former family for the sake of the children. Weddings, bar mitzvahs, and graduations should be happy occasions. Don't spoil them.

5. Capitalize on the positive side of your new relationship. Don't place unrealistic expectations or demands on your new mate. It is unreasonable to expect another human being to meet all your needs. Avoid criticizing or continually comparing your new partner unfavorably with your former spouse.

6. It sometimes takes months or even years to adjust to a new set of living patterns, dietary habits, and the likes and dislikes of a new partner. Be open to sharing novel experiences, as well as foods, entertainment habits, and other activities.

7. Talk out your problems this time around. Don't permit unspoken resentments to grow and fester. Open communication should begin

long before your trip to the altar and continue throughout your marriage.

8. Be sensitive to wounds and scars inflicted by the previous partner. Reassure your mate, particularly in areas that were troublesome in the former marriage. Don't tease or kid about things that may seem trivial to you but that are painful to your spouse.

9. You are beginning with a clean slate. Take full advantage of your fresh start. Your new partner does not have the preconceived notions that may have stifled your growth before. This is your chance to explore new opportunities, go back to school, change your career, and discover unaccustomed and stimulating interests for perhaps the first time in your life.

The Men's-Rights Movement

14

The men's-rights movement has not experienced the same support and growth as have women's groups. It is unfortunate that men have been taught to keep their problems and emotions to themselves. There has been a general lack of concern for the well-being of males in our society. Many groups have emerged which address the overt problems of women. But the difficulties men face are more subtle and are often treated lightly by society and by men themselves.

However, at last men are beginning to realize that they are an oppressed minority and that they face problems both within themselves and in the way they are treated by others. A new male consciousness is emerging, out of which are growing men's- and fathers'-rights groups all across the country. At present there are only a few hundred men's-rights groups available to help men with their problems.

As yet there is no strong national organization which addresses the economic, legal and emotional needs of men. But men's awakening recognition of their plight, together with a backlash to the strident demands of some female activists, is sowing the seeds for a strong men's-rights movement.

The men's-rights movement is more than a mirror image of the women's movement. The men's movement has a unique color of its own and addresses the male experience. Men have become aware that a strong national women's movement will not in and of itself solve men's problems. In fact, many of the demands women are making are made at the expense of men.

Much of the legislation that women are pushing has worked against men. The national parent-locator system is used to ferret out men who are not paying their child support. But it is not used to find women who have disappeared with the children.

Women's-rights activists have fostered an unequal administration of justice. The district attorney's office is used as a collection agency for child-support payments, but district attorneys refuse to help men "collect" their visitation rights.

Female leaders have been conspicuous by their absence from the fight for joint-custody laws. But they are very much in view when a wage-assignment bill for alimony or child support is pending. These same women speak out on abortion, paternity, and alimony issues which favor only their cause.

However, there are many women who do recognize the merit in the men's-rights cause. Some of the most militant supporters of the men's movement are second wives, sweethearts, and grandmothers who have seen the shabby treatment given their husbands, boyfriends, and sons.

There are hundreds of groups scattered throughout the country. A list of these organizations is included in the Appendix. They vary in size and makeup and are dedicated to divorce reform and men's rights. These men and women are working systematically and rationally to change unfair laws and to expose the inequities in our court system and in society in general.

How Men's-Rights Groups Work

Most organizations provide help and support on a one-to-one basis to men in the throes of divorce. These groups are also instrumental in backing legislation and changing laws which are unfair to men. They work to see that laws are implemented in the courts after they have been passed. The following are some of the services and types of assistance which many men's-rights organizations provide.

Court monitoring. Court-monitoring programs serve two functions. They provide an opportunity to observe a divorce court in action. As a court monitor, a prospective litigant can watch how judges and attorneys behave in the courtroom. A courtroom can be an intimidating and threatening place for the uninitiated. Monitoring someone else's trial can help make a man more comfortable when his case is heard.

A second function of court monitoring is to apprise the community of unfair and unfit judges. Some men's-rights groups encourage their members to observe judges in action and make objective notes on their performance. This information is collated and reported to members. Reports are given concerning the percentage of custody awards to women, unfair alimony amounts, contempt citations, and so forth.

Many men feel court monitors have a positive effect on judges. The presence of a row of neatly dressed, note-taking men and women, wearing badges which read "Court Monitor," forces many judges to truly consider the fairness of their decisions.

Visitation-violation witnesses. Group members are sometimes asked to serve as witnesses to visitation violations. They appear with a father on his appointed visitation day and observe the behavior of the parties. Objective observers may testify later if the father brings a contempt citation against his ex-spouse for abusing his visitation rights.

Group-therapy sessions. Some men's-rights

groups hold regular meetings and encourage members to communicate their feelings openly and share their experiences, frustrations and fears. They provide a supportive environment where a member can vent his feelings without recrimination. For many men this is their first opportunity to openly talk about their divorce or hostile feelings they have toward a spouse or attorney. It's a place to let off steam and get a sympathetic ear.

Soon some of these men begin bringing their new wives or sweethearts to meetings. They meet other couples with common problems and interests. For some men this is the beginning of a new life.

Crisis hotline. Several fathers'-rights and men's-rights organizations maintain twenty-four-hour crisis hotlines. These phones are staffed by men and women who understand the difficulties men face when they are going through divorce or have custody and visitation problems. These volunteers provide a sympathetic ear and often help avoid violent confrontations or other destructive behavior.

Referral attorneys. Many groups maintain lists of qualified family-law attorneys. These people are often very sensitive to men's problems in family-law matters. Some of these attorneys come to meetings regularly and speak on legal problems, court orders, and attorney-client relations.

Publication of newsletters. Numerous men's-rights groups publish newsletters which are mailed to members, the media, mental-health professionals and legislators. They report on a variety of topics, including legal matters, psychological problems of divorce, and current research and legislation.

Media and public-relations efforts. Some groups have been very effective in changing the attitudes of judges and attorneys through an active public-relations program. Men's-rights advocates appear on radio and television shows and write articles for local newspapers. In this way they inform the community of divorce inequities, the plight of disenfranchised fathers, and other family-law matters which require attention.

Lectures and seminars. Attorneys, judges and mental-health professionals are often invited to meetings sponsored by men's- and fathers'-rights groups. Couples who have made joint custody work after bitter court battles are favorite speakers.

Dissemination of information. Attorney checklists, handout sheets, and do's and don't's for men going through divorce are sometimes prepared and distributed. Men's-rights groups also circulate information on the legal system, mediation and arbitration alternatives, and new pieces of legislation. Some organizations maintain lending libraries of books and legal periodicals. Often the most authoritative and up-to-date source of current legislation and case law regarding divorce and custody is a men's-rights organization.

Demonstrations. Some groups take to the

streets when all else fails. They picket court-
houses, judges, district attorneys, or others
who exhibit blatant bias against men and fathers. These protests bring public pressure to
bear on the system.

One irate and frustrated Disneyland Dad pa-
raded in a black robe on the doorstep of the local courthouse, carrying a sign which read
"Every day is Ladies' Day with me." His picture hit all the papers and generated a lot of
interest.

Few attorneys will risk the wrath of a judge
by criticizing the status quo, and it is the rare
judge who will institute reform from within.
Therefore men's-rights advocates are in a
unique position to constructively critique the
legal system.

Sponsoring legislation. Some men's-rights
groups engage in active lobbying and legislative efforts. Several states have passed joint-
custody legislation as a result of efforts on the
part of group members. Equal enforcement of
visitation rights, reasonable alimony and child
support, equitable property settlements, and
preventing removal of children from a jurisdiction are high on the list of legislative priorities.

Men As People

One of the most important aspects of the men's-
rights movement is the sensitization of judges

and the legal system to the fact that men are people, that they feel pain, rejection, and experience deep-seated loss at the separation from their homes and families.

Judges and attorneys are finally beginning to really listen to men and to see them as more than mere litigants or adversaries. This change in attitude is slowly starting to make itself felt across the country. Hopefully the day will soon come when men are treated with equality in the courtroom and when fathering is valued as much as mothering by society.

When joint custody is given as a matter of course, when women no longer look upon men as their protectors and keepers during marriage and as their insurance policies after divorce, then men's-rights groups can happily vote themselves out of existence.

Appendix

1981 Single Dad's Lifestyle
Blue List of Father's Rights
and Divorce Reform Organizations

A message from Robert A. Hirschfeld, Editor and Publisher, *Single Dad's Lifestyle:*

The Blue List is published as a service to divorcing/divorced fathers everywhere. *Single Dad's Lifestyle* maintains a 24-hour hotline (602-998-0980) to help Dads nationwide locate resources such as the Blue Listed organizations in their local areas. While every effort has been made to provide accurate listings, there are inevitable obsolete addresses or phone numbers, and *Single Dad's Lifestyle* periodically publishes updates in its pages during the year.

ALASKA

Family Law Reform & Justice
    Council of Alaska
Rudy Johnson
Post Office Box 4-1646
Anchorage, Alaska 99509
(907) 333-6693

Mom's House and Dad's House
c/o Marko Lewis
Box 136
Hyder, Alaska 99923

ALABAMA

Alabama Federation of Fathers
Dothan/Troy Enterprise
Ron Smith
Post Office Box 448
Elba, Alabama 36323
(205) 347-4266

Alabama Federation of Fathers
Frank Varnell
Post Office Box 2773
Muscle Shoals, Alabama 35660
(205) 381-4496

Alabama Federation of Fathers
Dave Petersen
Post Office Box 744
Huntsville, Alabama 35804
(205) 723-4349

ARIZONA

Association for Fathers And
    Children Together (AFACT)
Dan Malatesta
Post Office Box 1428
Phoenix, Arizona 85001
Hotline: (602) 956-7999

Single Dad's Lifestyle
Subscriptions: $12 per year
Post Office Box 4842
Scottsdale, Arizona 85261
Hotline: (602) 998-0980

ARKANSAS

Arkansas Fathers for Equal
    Rights/Wives & Grandparents
Dr. David S. McCray, President
Post Office Box 5701
Brady Station
Little Rock, Arkansas 72215
(501) 661-5800/ofc.
(501) 663-3116/home

CALIFORNIA

Equal Rights for Fathers, Bay
    Area
Post Office Box 6327
Albany, California 94706
(415) 848-2323

Equal Rights for Fathers,
  Sacramento
Dr. A.D. Adins
Post Office Box 161323
Sacramento, California 95814
(916) 422-8888

Equal Rights for Fathers, Marin
Alva Wooley
Post Office Box 337
Novato, California 94948
(415) 459-4019

Help Abolish Legal Tyranny
(HALT of California)
Stan Faust
Post Office Box 50034
Palo Alto, California 94303
(415) 856-4528

Family Law Action Council
Howard P. Jeter
Post Office Box 3213
Berkeley, California 94706
(415) 841-7839

National Counseling Center
Mel Krantzler
610 D Street
San Rafael, California 94901
(415) 454-7770

*Nurturing News: A Forum for
  Men in the Lives of Children*
Subscription: $5/year (4 issues)
David Giveans, Editor
187 Caselli Avenue
San Francisco, California 94114
(415) 861-0847

United States Divorce Reform
George Partis
Post Office Box 243
Kenwood, California 95452
(707) 833-4470

California Men's-Rights Coalition
Gerald A. Silver, Coordinator
Post Office Box 7596
Van Nuys, California 91409
(213) 789-4435

Fathers' Aid of San Diego
George Grider
Post Office Box 80914
San Diego, California 92138
(714) 225-1807

Joint Custody Association
c/o James Cook
10606 Wilkins Avenue
Los Angeles, California 90024
(213) 772-4200

Fathers' Rights of America, Inc.
Gerald A. Silver
Post Office Box 7596
Van Nuys, California 91409
(213) 789-4435

Parents Anonymous
22330 Hawthorne
  Boulevard, #208
Torrance, California 90505
(213) 371-3501

Fathers Demanding Equal
 Justice
Vert Vergon
3752 Motor Avenue
Los Angeles, California 90034
(213) 836-1997

In Pro Per
John Adair
Post Office Box 3374
Huntington Park, California
(213) 582-1929

Fathers United for Equal Justice
David Weick
Post Office Box 17173
Irvine, California 92713
(714) 598-9329

Family Law Action Council
Dr. Carlo E. Abruzzeze
Post Office Box 6168
Santa Ana, California 92706
(714) 499-1966

United Fathers' Organization of
 America National Divorce
Rod Bivings
The Spurgeon Building
206 West 4th Street,
 Room 435
Santa Ana, California 92706
(714) 542-5624

Divorce Aid, Inc.
Clint Jones
24991 Via Portola
Laguna Niguel, California 92677
(714) 831-9644

COLORADO

Fathers' Rights
Karl Danninger
Post Office Box 3125
Boulder, Colorado 80307
(303) 447-9517

American Families Together with
 Equal Responsibilities (AFTER)
Harold Pyper, Sr.
7717 Quivas
Denver, Colorado 80221
(303) 427-1845

CONNECTICUT

Divorced Men's Association of
 Connecticut
Bob Adams
Box 723
Waterbury, Connecticut 06720
(203) 528-0526

Divorced Men's Association of
 Connecticut
Rudy Tomasik
Box 95
S. Woodstock, Connecticut
 06267

National Committee for Fair
 Divorce Laws
Julian Langer
86 St. Charles Street
Stamford, Connecticut 06907

Connecticut Conference on
   Child Custody
Christine Albrecht
Post Office Box 194
Plantsville, Connecticut 06479

Family Mediation Association
5018 Allan Road
Washington, DC 20016
Main Office (301) 320-3300
Capitol Hill Office
   (202) 547-6693

DELAWARE

Male Parents for Equal Rights
Thomas Alexander
1739 West 5th Street
Wilmington, Delaware 19805
(302) 571-8383

FLORIDA

United Fathers, Inc.
Dade County Chapter
Jerry Clark
(305) 251-3000

DISTRICT OF COLUMBIA

United Fathers, Inc.
Broward County Chapter
William Guarro
1425 South East 17th Street
Fort Lauderdale, Florida 33316
(305) 527-4162

Help Abolish Legal Tyranny
   (HALT)
201 Massachusetts Avenue
   N. E., Suite 319
Washington, DC 20002

Children's Rights, Inc.,
   National Headquarters
(Anti-custodial-kidnapping
   organization)
Arnold Miller
3443 17th Street N. W.
Washington, DC 20010
(202) 462-7573

United Fathers, Inc.
Fort Walton Chapter
Larry Patrick
234 North Eglin Parkway
Fort Walton Beach, Florida
   32548
(904) 244-7181

Fathers United Demanding
   Equal Justice
Dr. Harold Goldstein
8121 South West 81st Court
Miami, Florida 33143

Parents Without Partners, Inc.
Legal Research Committee
7910 Woodmont Avenue
Washington, DC 20014

Florida Dads for Fairness in
Custody
Dr. Ken Schultz
9020 North West 8th Street,
Apartment 521
Miami, Florida 33172

National Society of Fathers for
Child Custody/Divorce Law
Reform
Ed. Winter, Jr.
Post Office Box 010847
Flagler Station
Miami, Florida 33137
(305) 371-5225

Rights of Second Spouses
Nancy Postal Williams
1940 South West 46 Terrace
Fort Lauderdale, Florida 33317

Florida Divorce Association
Mark Austin
Box 5597
Jacksonville, Florida 32207

Equal Rights for Dads and Single
Parents Justice League
Robert D. Hertz
3301 North East 5th Avenue,
418
Miami, Florida 33137
(305) 576-3117

Equal Rights in Court for Dads
Jim Roy
500 North West 9th Street
Fort Lauderdale, Florida 33311

Florida Fathers for Equal Rights
Gerry Mooney
Post Office Box 610461
Miami, Florida 33161

Citizen's Legal Protective
League
Dr. Merle E. Parker
Post Office Box 2031
Sanford, Florida 32725

GEORGIA

Consumers of Legal Services
Post Office Box 223
Duraville, Georgia 30340
(404) 964-0992/458-4969

Stabilize the Home/Save the
Child
John M. Barber
1630 Springbrook Drive
Decatur, Georgia 30033
(404) 491-7332

Family Mediation Association
O.J. Coogler, J.D.
2559 Piedmont Road N. E.
Atlanta, Georgia 30305
(404) 262-1900

Single Dad's Research Project
Dr. Rand D. Conger, Ph.D.
Department of Sociology
University of Georgia
Athens, Georgia 30602

ILLINOIS

Citizens for Constitutional Rights
Richard M. Boalby
512 23rd Street
Post Office Box 1456
Rock Island, Illinois 61201
(309) 786-1478

F.A.T.H.E.R.
Charles Brown
Post Office Box 49314
Chicago, Illinois 60649

American Divorce Association
  Men (ADAM)
Louis Filczer
1008 White Oak Street
Arlington Heights, Illinois 60005
(312) 870-1040

American Family
  Communiversity
Les Kohut
5242 W. North Avenue
Chicago, Illinois 60639
(312) 236-3946

American Society of Divorced
  Men (ASDM)
Richard Templeton
575 Keep Street
Elgin, Illinois 60020
(312) 695-2200

Citizens for Constitutional
  Courts
Joe J. Adams
23 Covington Road
Fox Lake, Illinois 60020
(312) 587-5350

Divorce Anonymous
Post Office Box 5313
Chicago, Illinois 60680
(312) 242-9325

Give the Courts Back to the
  People
Reverend Lawson Hall
2115 Gilead Avenue
Zion, Illinois 60099
(312) 872-3468

Committee to Clean Up the
  Courts
Sherman Skolnick
9800 South Oglesby Avenue
Chicago, Illinois 60617

INDIANA

Indiana Father's Alliance
Carl R. Cornell
4724 West Regent
Indianapolis, Indiana 46241
(317) 244-7322

Divorce Equality for All
Charles Schulz
302 South Arlington Avenue
Indianapolis, Indiana 46219

Fathers for Equal Rights
Lee Silen
Post Office Box 2028
Evansville, Indiana 47714

Fathers for Equal Rights
Richard & Niki Wayland
2724 Medford
LaFayette, Indiana 47905

Fathers for Equal Rights
Donald Schafer
2204 Summerfield Drive
LaFayette, Indiana 47905

Fathers for Equal Rights
Marshall & Pat Campbell
3724 Sugar Lane
Bloomington, Indiana 47401

IOWA

Divorce Reform Center
Don Lamb
Box 862
Marshalltown, Iowa 50158
(515) 753-8361

KANSAS

Fathers Demanding Equal
   Justice
Robert A. Woff
689 South Mission Road
Wichita, Kansas 67207
(316) 686-5871

Divorce Equality
1414 South Handley
Wichita, Kansas 67213

MAINE

Coalition Organized for Parental
   Equality (COPE)
Peter T. Cyr
68 Deering Street
Portland, Maine 04101

US Divorce Reform of Maine
Gilbert Stockton
138 Ocean Street
South Portland, Maine 04106
(207) 799-6812

MARYLAND

Fathers United for Equal Rights
Towson Chapter
Charles Biddison
Post Office Box 11243
Baltimore, Maryland 21239
(301) 433-5114

Fathers United for Equal Rights
Allen C. Thomas
Post Office Box 159
Columbia, Maryland 21045
(301) 997-4658

Fathers United for Equal Rights
Gary Sowers
Post Office Box 4944
Baltimore, Maryland 21220
(301) 574-9017
Hotline: (301) 686-4355

Fathers United for Equal Rights
John Davis
Post Office Box 3308
Silver Spring, Maryland 20901

Free Men (Anti-Sexism
   Organization)
Eugene V. Martin
Post Office Box 920
Columbia, Maryland 21044

American Man
Richard Haddad, Editor
Subscriptions: $14
Post Office Box 693
Columbia, Maryland 21045

National Committee for Citizens
  in Education (NCCE)
(Opposes divorced-parent
  discrimination)
410 Wilde Lake Village Green
Columbia, Maryland 21044

Equal Rights in Divorce, Inc.
Alfred Minner
Post Office Box 211
Clarksburg, Maryland 20734
(301) 428-0392

MASSACHUSETTS

Fighting Injustice Pro-Se
  Headquarters
Nat Denman
Box 689
Falmouth, Massachusetts 02541
(617) 548-3295

Fighting Injustice Pro-Se
Robert Silvia
50 Blaine Street
Brockton, Massachusetts 02401
(617) 584-6459

American Conference on
  Divorced and Separated
  Catholics
5 Park Street
Boston, Massachusetts 02108

Fathers Fight for Children
Jeanne Desmarais
Post Office Box 461
North Amherst, Massachusetts
  01059

Divorced Fathers for Action &
  Justice
Alfred Bonica
Post Office Box 323
Westboro, Massachusetts
  01581
(617) 891-5746

Divorced Parents for Justice
Bernard Harrington
Box 183
Cheshire, Massachusetts 01225
(413) 743-0583

Fathers United for Equal Justice
Robert Osler
339 Auburn Street
Auburndale, Massachusetts
  02116
(617) 965-5460

Divorced Fathers for Action
65 Mount Hope Street
Roslindale, Massachusetts
  02131

Umbilical Connection Men's
  Center
Riki Haney
635 Main Street
Amherst, Massachusetts 01002
(413) 256-6128

MICHIGAN

Fathers for Equal Rights of
   America
Wayne/Oakland/Macomb
   County
Alan Z. Lebow
30233 Southfield Road,
   Suite 208
Southfield, Michigan 48076
(313) 354-3080

Fathers for Equal Rights of
   America
Jackson County Chapter
Joseph T. Novak
Post Office Box 1303
Jackson, Michigan 49204
(517) 787-3916

Fathers for Equal Rights of
   America
Ann Arbor Chapter
Leigh Travis
861 Honey Creek Drive
Ann Arbor, Michigan 48013
(313) 761-3427

Fathers for Equal Rights of
   America
Ray Fogelsong
Port Huron, Michigan 48060
(313) 987-8268

Fathers for Equal Rights of
   America
Phyllis Waltz
4299 Beaverton Road
Beaverton, Michigan 48612
(517) 435-9224

Fathers for Equal Rights of
   America
Lansing Area Chapter
Cylene Baker
11624 Sunfield Highway
Sunfield, Michigan 48890
(517) 566-8205

Fathers Who Care
Morse Brown
Post Office Box 1256
Muskegon, Michigan 49443
(616) 722-3741

Equal Rights for Fathers of
   Michigan
Post Office Box 291
Westland, Michigan 48185
(313) 591-0419

Equal Rights for Fathers of
   Michigan
7200 Alger Drive
Davison, Michigan 48423
(313) 742-3403

Equal Rights for Fathers of
   Michigan
2210 Riverside Drive, Lot C-13
Saulte Saint Marie, Michigan
   49783
(906) 635-0690

Committee on Marriage &
   Divorce (CMAD)
Max W. Lemmon
Post Office Box 1072
Mt. Clemens, Michigan 48043
(313) 749-5256

MINNESOTA

US Divorce Reform of
    Minnesota
Charles VanDuzee
11702 Cartier Avenue
Burnsville, Minnesota 55337
(612) 894-7200

Men's Equality Now,
    International
Richard Doyle
Post Office Box 189
Forest Lake, Minnesota 55025
(612) 464-7663

Divorce Education Association
Chuck Thibodeau
3955 Upton Avenue South
South Minneapolis, Minnesota
    55410
(612) 926-4003

MISSOURI

Divorced Dads,
A Fight for Equal Rights, Inc.
Jack D. Paradise
9229 Ward Parkway, Suite 250
Kansas City, Missouri 64114
(816) 333-9911

National Association of Christian
    Singles
Donald Davidson
Post Office Box 11394
Kansas City, Missouri 64112
(816) 763-9401

NEBRASKA

DADS of America
Kurt Freiberg
618 South 113th Avenue
Omaha, Nebraska 68154
(402) 333-7509

NEVADA

Fathers for Equal Justice
Joe De Beauchamp
Post Office Box 15422
Las Vegas, Nevada 89114
(701) 735-4104

NEW HAMPSHIRE

Fathers United for Equal Justice
Fred Hoyt
New Hampshire College,
    Box 555
2500 North River Road
Manchester, New Hampshire
    03104
(603) 622-3039/889-0657/
    746-3525/889-7051

Fathers United for Equal Rights
17 Ministerial Road
Bedford, New Hampshire 03102

NEW JERSEY

Fathers United for Equal Rights
Somerset County
Post Office Box 6066
Bridgewater, New Jersey 08807
(201) 526-6308

Fathers United for Equal Rights
Marshall Resnick
Post Office Box 83
Milltown, New Jersey 08850
(201) 736-0576

Fathers United for Equal Rights
Monmouth County
George Woodward
Post Office Box 374
Red Bank, New Jersey 07701
(201) 493-2792

Father's United for Equal Rights
Passaic County
Vince Bologna
28 Ann Street
Wayne, New Jersey 07470
(201) 694-3238

Men's Pro Se Legal Awareness
28 Ann Street
Wayne, New Jersey 07470
(201) 694-3238

National Congress for Men
Joseph A. Barbier
Post Office Box 147
Mendham, New Jersey 07945
(201) 696-7030

Dissatisfied Divorced Men
Harry M. Feller, Jr.
Post Office Box 231
Titusville, New Jersey 08560

Family Law Council
Anthony Gil
Post Office Box 217
Fair Lawn, New Jersey 07410
(201) 696-5156

Alimony, Inc.
John A. Becker
Post Office Box 9
Columbus, New Jersey 08022

Together, Inc.
7 State Street
Glassboro, New Jersey 08028
(609) 881-4040

NEW MEXICO

Divorced American Men Unite
Mike & Judy Gadler
2436 Black Mesa Loop S. W.
Albuquerque, New Mexico
87105
(505) 877-8721

NEW YORK

Equal Rights for Fathers of NYS
Gary Brown
Post Office Box 546
Rochester, New York 14602
(716) 544-1193

Equal Rights for Fathers of NYS
John Rossler
3715 Brewerton Road
North Syracuse, New York
13212
(315) 455-7043
(315) 471-1953

Equal Rights for Fathers of NYS
Bruce Gerling
Post Office Box 225
New Hartford, New York 13413
(315) 593-7121

Equal Rights for Fathers of NYS
Al Lefkowitz
4651 Watkins Road
Pine Valley, New York 14872

Equal Rights for Fathers of NYS
Wesley Moore
1511 Rugby Road
Schenectady, New York 12308
(518) 377-7987

Equal Rights for Fathers of NYS
John Couture
1096 Cleveland
Cheektowaga, New York 14225

Equal Rights for Fathers of NYS
Phillip Smith
1038 42nd Street
Brooklyn, New York 11219
(212) 854-4036

Equal Rights for Fathers of NYS
Ken Dibble, Jr.
Box 3
Hartwick, New York 13348

League for Equal Justice and
   Human Rights in Divorce and
   Legal Separation
Dr. M. Radh Achuthan
Post Office Box 985
Southampton, New York 11968
(516) 283-5010

Father's Rights
William D. Nye
365 Girard Avenue
East Aurora, New York 14502
(716) 652-5528

Fathers for Equal Rights
Dr. Robert E. Fay, M.D.
19 North Belmont Circle
Oneonta, New York 13820

United Parents and Fathers for
   Divorce Law Fairness
Raymond N. Palmer
13-20 143rd Place
Whitestone, New York 11357

Children's Rights, Inc.
(Anti-custodial-kidnapping
   organization)
John Gill
19 Maple Avenue
Stony Brook, New York 11790
(516) 751-7840

National Committee of Fair
   Divorce/Alimony Laws, Inc.
George Dunbar
Box 641, Lenox Hill Station
New York, New York 10021
(212) 879-8945

Men for ERA
Robert Bennett
152 Lisbon
Buffalo, New York 14214

Deprived and Discriminated-
Against Males
Norman Kopp
102 South Main Street
North Syracuse, New York
13212

United Parents & Fathers for
Divorce Law Fairness
Raymond N. Palmer
13-20 143rd Place
Whitestone, New York 11357

NORTH DAKOTA

North Dakota Fathers for Equal
Rights
Murray Muraskin
907 24th Avenue South
Grand Forks, North Dakota
58201
(701) 746-5452

OHIO

Trumbull Fathers for Equal
Justice
Jerry Brest
89 Indianola Road
Boardman, Ohio 44512
(216) 782-0347

Parents for Equal Justice/
Northwest Ohio
Bob Feiklowicz
Post Office Box 6481
Toledo, Ohio 43623
(419) 478-6600
Hotline: (419) 473-0333

Fathers for Equal Justice/
Northeast Ohio
Bill Burgess
Post Office Box 6868
Cleveland, Ohio 44101
(216) 861-6868

Columbus Fathers for Equal
Justice
Donn Griffith
3859 West Dublin-Granville Road
Dublin, Ohio 43017
(614) 889-2558

OREGON

Non-Custodial Parents
Association
Victor Smith
Attention: Oshatz, 6th Floor
Concord Building
Portland, Oregon 97204
(503) 228-2244

Custodial Father's Association of
Douglas County
Ron Lewis
Post Office Box 223
Wilbur, Oregon 97494

Oregon Divorce Reform
Association
Greg Ripke
Post Office Box 765
Newport, Oregon 97365
(503) 265-8849

PENNSYLVANIA

Father's and Children's Equality
  FACE: Greater Philadelphia
  Chapter
Ken Delmar
Post Office Box 117
Drexel Hill, Pennsylvania 19026
(215) 688-4748

FACE: Western Chapter
Bill Thompson
637 Garden City Drive
Monroeville, Pennsylvania
  15146
(412) 373-3031

FACE: Central Chapter
Dr. Meryl Arnold
Box 93
Saxton, Pennsylvania 16678
(814) 635-2379

FACE: Eastern Chapter
Ed Urbanski
Box 149
Lake Wunda, Pennsylvania
  18625

FACE: Allegheny County
Lou Baler
603 Carrara Drive
Allison Park, Pennsylvania
  15101
(412) 486-3166

FACE: Butler County
John H. Nagy
Post Office Box 2012
Butler, Pennsylvania 16001
(412) 287-1683

FACE: Chester County
Al Wojtowicz
40 Mary Fran Drive
Westchester, Pennsylvania
  19380
(215) 436-9543

FACE: Dauphin County
Gordon Warfel
2333 North 2nd Street
Harrisburg, Pennsylvania 17110
(717) 234-3479

FACE: Elk County
Andrew Marconi
102 Bayberry Road
Saint Mary's, Pennsylvania
  15857
(814) 834-2801

FACE: Lebanon County
Steve Resneski
2902 Pineford Drive
Middletown, Pennsylvania
  17057
(717) 944-2150

FACE: Lycoming Chapter
Gerald Caputo
1503 High Street
Williamsport, Pennsylvania
  17701

FACE: Perry County
David Patton
207 Greenwood Street
Box 93
Millerstown, Pennsylvania 17062

FACE: Philadelphia County
John Gill
12504 Fedor Place
Philadelphia, Pennsylvania
19154
(215) 632-3053

FACE: York/Lancaster
Bradley Rinehart
1508 Stanton Street
York, Pennsylvania 17404
(717) 846-6066

Divorce and Child Custody
Mediation Services, Inc.
Veronica Steadle
1170 Wyoming Avenue
Forty Fort, Pennsylvania 18704
(717) 287-1248

National Council of Marriage and
Divorce Law Reform and
Justice Organizations; Family
Law Reform and Justice
Council
George F. Doppler
Post Office Box 60
Broomall, Pennsylvania 19008
(215) 353-3462

Child Custody Evaluation
Service
Dr. Ken Lewis
Post Office Box 202-Dept. SDL
Glenside, Pennsylvania 19038
(215) 576-0177

Fathers United for Equal Rights
John C. Ermel
Post Office Box 743
Pittston, Pennsylvania 18640
(717) 654-2852

Fathers United for Equal Rights
Charles S. Hanna
6271 Hill Drive
Wescosville, Pennsylvania 18106
(215) 395-6469

Fathers United for Equal Rights
Jerry Solomon
3 Green Ridge Street
Scranton, Pennsylvania 18508
(717) 587-0393

Father's Association to Help
Establish Reform (FATHER) of
Pittsburgh
RD#1, Box 294
Hookstown, Pennsylvania
15050

Council on Fair Family Law
Cole Y. Gittman
2215 Green Street
Chester, Pennsylvania 19013
(215) 522-7122

Fathers for Fair Support
RD#2, Box 200
Conneaut Lake, Pennsylvania
16316
(814) 382-2986

Divorced Dads for Justice
Alan R. Baumann
Post Office Box 97
Horsham, Pennsylvania 19044

Citizen's League on Custody
    and Kidnapping
Chris Gallagher
Post Office Box 1991
Norwood, Pennsylvania 19074

Fathers United for Equal Rights
Lehigh Valley Chapter
Jack Conwell
1259 South Jefferson Street
Allentown, Pennsylvania 18103
(215) 791-2187

Fathers United for Equal Rights
Paul Zylis
Post Office Box 1676
Kingston, Pennsylvania 18704
(717) 378-2033

RHODE ISLAND

Fathers United for Equal Justice
Reverend Gerald Gordon
48 Campbell Avenue
Rumford, Rhode Island 02914
(401) 434-7201

Single Father's Study &
    Research
Dr. Henry Biller
Dept. of Psychology
University of Rhode Island
Kingston, Rhode Island 02881

TENNESSEE

Father's Rights, Inc.
Alan E. Moore
625 Brister, #21
Memphis, Tennessee 38111
(901) 324-9271

TEXAS

Texas Fathers for Equal Rights
Bill Swearingen
Post Office Box 79670
Houston, Texas 77079
(713) 960-0407

Texas Fathers for Equal Rights
Hollis Grizzard
Post Office Box 10281
San Antonio, Texas 78210
(512) 337-6803

Texas Fathers for Equal Rights
Post Office Box 3603
Austin, Texas 78764
(512) 442-5336

Texas Fathers for Equal Rights
Jack Weller
Post Office Box 50052
Dallas, Texas 75250
(214) 934-3885

Men's Equality Now
Donald R. Beagle
612 South Twin City Highway
Nederlands, Texas 77627
(713) 722-0734

UTAH

Utah Father's Protective
  Association
Jack Ford
1240 East Mount View Drive
Smithfield, Utah 84335
(801) 563-5062

National Legal Foundation for
  Protection of Parents &
  Children's Rights
c/o Peter Guyon, Esquire
820 Newhouse Building
Salt Lake City, Utah 84111

VIRGINIA

Fathers United for Equal Rights
Elliot Diamond
4611 Columbia Pike
Post Office Box 1323
Arlington, Virginia 22210
(703) 892-1777

Fathers United for Equal Rights
Mike Riley
4609 Clifford Street
Portsmouth, Virginia 23707
(804) 394-5367

United States Divorce Reform
Donald Clevenger
809 West Broad Street,
  Apartment 118
Falls Church, Virginia 24147

Divorced Male Parents for
  Equal Justice
Ralph M. Halliwill
Post Office Box 307
Rich Creek, Virginia 24147

Divorce Seminars
David I. Levine
Post Office Box 880
Portsmouth, Virginia 23705
(804) 399-4061

WASHINGTON

US Divorce Reform of
  Washington
Guy Moats
Post Office Box 693
Bellevue, Washington 98009
(206) 235-0528

US Divorce Reform of Tacoma
Richard Wittman
Post Office Box 8111
Tacoma, Washington 98408
(206) 473-1598

US Divorce Reform of Kent
Mary Munoz
Post Office Box 553
Kent, Washington 98031

US Divorce Reform of
  Wenatchee
Rich Waller
3500 5th. North East #1
East Wenatchee, Washington
  98801

Fighting Injustice Pro-Se
Robert Karls
Post Office Box 55443
Seattle, Washington 98155
(206) 362-6229

WISCONSIN

Wisconsin Father's Alliance
Children's Legal Defenders
Ken Pangborn
811 South 36th Street
Milwaukee, Wisconsin 53215
(414) 645-3360

Wisconsin Institute on Divorce
Lee Haydock
Post Office Box 1905
Milwaukee, Wisconsin 53201
(414) 383-4159

INTERNATIONAL LISTINGS

Defence Against Women's
   Maintenance & Alimony
Morris Revelman
Box 76, Post Office Brighton,
Victoria 3186, AUSTRALIA

Alimony Anonymous
Candy Smith
Post Office Box 1904
New Liskeard, Ontario POJ 1PO
CANADA

Society of Single Fathers
Nillo Piccinin
38 Wilkinson Drive
Willowdale, Ontario M2J 3Z5
CANADA
(416) 496-2899

Society of Single Fathers
Myron Balych
2219 Smith Street
Regina, Saskatchewan S4P 2P5
CANADA
(306) 522-9759

Divorce Law Reform Union
R.V. Banks, Chairman
"Savernake", 121 Ashford
   Road
Bearstead, Nr. Maidstone, Kent
ENGLAND

Families Need Fathers
John Bell, Farnborough 54345
39 Cloonmore Avenue
Orpington, Kent BR6 9LE
ENGLAND

Families Need Fathers
Sheila Burns
97-C Shakespeare Walk
London N16 8TB ENGLAND
Tel:01-254-6680

Family Law Reform Association
Eric Giles
34 Talhot Crescent
Chesterfield, Derbyshire
ENGLAND

National Children's Bureau
Mia Kellmer Pringle, Director
8 Wakeley Street
Islington, London EC1V 7QE
ENGLAND
Tel: 01-278-9441-7

Mouvement de la Conditions
Masculine et Paternelle
Jean-Luc Schmerber
181 Rue des Courcelles
75017 Paris, FRANCE
754-5505

Divorced Father's Association
Menahem Aharoni, Secretary
Post Office Box 668
Tel-Aviv, ISRAEL

MEN'S International
Salvatore Capalbo
c/o A.V.V. Piazza Mazzini 8,
Rome 00195 ITALY

Gunnar Berling, General
  Secretary
Barnefedrenes Nordiske Rad
Postoks 2485, Solli, NORWAY

Selected Readings

For anyone who wants to become knowledgeable on the subjects of divorce, child custody, and men's rights, these books will be helpful. The authors do not necessarily endorse all of the opinions in these books.

Atkins, Edith, and Rubin, Estelle. *Part-Time Father: A Guide for the Divorced Father.* New American Library (1977) $1.75.

Bienenfeld, Florence. *My Mom and Dad Are Getting a Divorce.* EMC Corporation (1980) $3.95.

Blackwell, Robert. *The Fighter's Guide to Divorce.* Contemporary Books (1979) $4.95.

Freud, Anna; Goldstein, Joseph; and Solnit, Albert. *Beyond the Best Interests of the Child.* Free Press (1973) $3.95.

Galper, Miriam. *The Joint Custody & Co-Parenting Handbook.* Running Press (1980) $5.95.

Goldberg, Herb. *The Hazards of Being Male.* New American Library (1977) $2.25.

Goldberg, Herb. *The New Male: From Self-Destruction to Self-Care.* New American Library (1980) $2.95.

Goldman, Gerald, and Shepard, Morris A. *Divorced Dads*. A Berkley Book (1980) $2.50.

Haddad, William, and Roman, Mel. *The Disposable Parent*. Penguin Books (1979) $3.95.

Hunt, Bernice, and Hunt, Morton. *The Divorce Experience*. New American Library (1979) $2.50.

Kahan, Stuart. *For Divorced Fathers Only.* Sovereign Books (1979) $3.95.

Kelly, Joan B., and Wallerstein, Judith S. *Surviving the Breakup: How Children & Parents Cope with Divorce*. Basic Books (1980) $18.50.

Keshet, Harry F., and Rosenthal, Kristine M. *Fathers Without Partners: A Study of Fathers & the Family After Marital Separation*. Rowman & Littlefield (1980) $15.95.

Krantzler, Mel. *Creative Divorce*. New American Library (1975) $2.25.

Nichols, Jack. *Men's Liberation: A New Definition of Masculinity.* Penguin Books (1975) $2.95.

Ricci, Isolina. *Mom's House, Dad's House: Making Shared Custody Work*. Macmillan (1980) $10.95.

Robertson, Christina. *Divorce & Decision-Making: A Woman's Guide*. Follett (1980) $7.95.

Vail, Lauren O. *Divorce: The Man's Complete Guide to Winning*. Sovereign Books (1979) $9.95.

Vanton, Monte. *Marriage—Grounds for Divorce*. Simon & Schuster (1979) $10.00.

Ware, Ciji. *Joint Custody: One Way to End the War.* Viking Press (forthcoming).

Wheeler, Michael. *Divided Children: A Legal Guide for Divorcing Parents.* Penguin Books (1981) $4.95.

Wishard, Bill, and Wishard, Laurie. *Men's Rights: A Handbook for the 80's.* Cragmont Publications (1980) $6.95.

Woolley, Persia. *The Custody Handbook.* Summit Books (1980) $5.95.

Newsletters

American Man. Post Office Box 693, Columbia, Maryland 21045.

Nurturing News: A Forum for Men in the Lives of Children. 187 Caselli Avenue, San Francisco, California 94114.

Single Dad's Lifestyle. Post Office Box 4842, Scottsdale, Arizona 85258.

Bibliography

"Alimony Claim? It'll Slay You!" *Los Angeles Times*, 2 May 1978.

Farley, Ellen. "For Richer: Lawsuits Bloom After the Living In." *Philadelphia Inquirer*, 30 July 1978.

Huerta, Loretta Kuklinsky. "Joint Custody: Co-Parenting After Divorce." *Los Angeles Times*, 30 January 1979.

Kelly, Joan B., and Wallerstein, Judith S. "California's Children of Divorce." *Psychology Today* (January 1980) p. 67.

Lebbos, Betsy Warren, and Trombetta, Diane, Ph.D. "Co-Parenting: The Best Custody Solution." *Los Angeles Daily Journal* 79:12 (22 June 1979) p. 11.

Marks, Marlene Adler. "Pal-imony: A Brand New Nightmare for L.A.'s Swingers." *Los Angeles* (October 1977) p. 140.

McDonald, Laughlin. "Speaking of Incompetence, Chief, What About Judges?" *Juris Doctor*, May 1978.

"Problems Found for Children With One Parent." *Roanoke Times & World News*, 9 August 1980.

"Producer Will Pay Wife $6,000 Monthly Support." *Los Angeles Times*, 29 June 1977.

Roman, Melvin, Ph.D. "The Disposable Parent." *Conciliation Courts Review* 15:2 (December 1977) p. 1.

Sanoff, Alvin P. "Welfare State Promotes What It Is Supposed to Cure: A Conversation With George Gilder." *U.S. News & World Report* (6 April 1981) pp. 53–54.

Seal, Karen, Ph.D. "A Decade of No-Fault Divorce: What It Has Meant Financially for Women in California." *Family Advocate* (Spring 1979) pp. 10–15.

Seligman, Joel. "Lawyer Incompetence: Greater Than Charged?" *Los Angeles Times*, 23 May 1978.

Spock, Benjamin, M.D. "Joint Custody and the Father's Role." *Redbook* (October 1979) pp. 77–79.